THE STORY OF
PORSCHE

Published in 2022 by Welbeck
An imprint of Welbeck Non-Fiction Limited,
Part of Welbeck Publishing Group.
Based in London and Sydney.
www.welbeckpublishing.com

Text © Welbeck Non-Fiction Limited, part of Welbeck Publishing Group.

All rights reserved. No part of this publication may be reproduced, stored in a retrieval system, or transmitted in any form or by any means, electronically, mechanical, photocopying, recording or otherwise, without the prior permission of the copyright owners and the publishers.

A CIP catalogue record for this book is available from the British Library.

ISBN 978 1 80279 291 1

Editors: Ross Hamilton & Conor Kilgallon
Design: Russell Knowles & Luana Gobbo
Picture Research: Paul Langan
Production: Rachel Burgess

Printed in China

10 9 8 7 6 5 4

Disclaimer:
All trademarks, images, quotations, company names, registered names, products, logos used or cited in this book are the property of their respective owners and are used in this book for identification, review and editorial purposes only. This book is a publication of Welbeck Non-Fiction Limited and has not been licensed, approved, sponsored, or endorsed by any person or entity and has no connection or association to Dr.-Ing. h.c. F. Porsche AG.

THE STORY OF
PORSCHE

A TRIBUTE TO THE
LEGENDARY MANUFACTURER

LUKE SMITH

CONTENTS

The House of Porsche 6

Out of the Ashes 24

The Birth of a Legend 46

Glory and Growing Pains 64

King of the Track 82

Revival Meets Rivalry 100

The Return to Le Mans 118

Electric Dreams 138

Index 156

Credits 160

THE HOUSE OF PORSCHE

SIGNS OF
GREATNESS

> "He is still very young, but he is a man with a great career ahead of him. You are going to hear a lot more from him. His name is Ferdinand Porsche."

When Ludwig Lohner made this proclamation at the Paris World Exhibition in 1900, he could not possibly have known just how prescient his words would prove.

More than a century later, the Porsche name has adorned millions of cars across the world, standing for the pinnacle of design and performance. Porsche has conquered the greatest racetracks in the world. Porsche changed the automotive industry forever.

But had he followed his father's wishes of working to one day take over his tinsmith business, Ferdinand Porsche may never have established the company that would go on to become such a global force and phenomenon.

Ferdinand Porsche was born to Anton and Anna Porsche in September 1875 in Maffersdorf, now known as Vratislavice in

OPPOSITE: A young Ferdinand Porsche, pictured during his time as a reserve foot soldier, had dreams from an early age of a career in engineering.

BELOW: A memorial plaque marks the birthplace of Ferdinand Porsche in Vratislavice, now part of the modern-day Czech Republic.

the modern-day Czech Republic. He showed an interest and aptitude for technology, particularly electricity, from a young age. With a view to take after his father, Ferdinand began a tinsmith apprenticeship at the age of 14, but became more and more interested in electrification – much to his father's disapproval.

Anna saw things differently. She encouraged Ferdinand to explore his interests as he experimented with rudimentary electrical devices in the attic of the family home, with one creation being ice skates featuring battery-powered lights. Anton was persuaded to allow Ferdinand to attend evening classes at a nearby technical college to study electrical engineering. At the age of 18, Ferdinand made the Porsche family home only the second building in Vratislavice to have electric lighting.

It quite literally proved to be a light-bulb moment that encouraged Ferdinand to further pursue his interests by moving to Vienna, where he started to transfer his skills into the automotive sphere. He joined the Egger electrical company, through which he would begin to work with Jacob Lohner and Co., a company that produced coaches and vehicles, and was now being run by Ludwig Lohner.

In 1898, with encouragement from Lohner, Porsche designed his first car. Although it looked more like a wooden cart that would be pulled along by horses, it was electric-powered and could reach speeds of up to 21 mph. Officially known as the Egger-Lohner C.2 Phaeton, the car is largely remembered as the 'Porsche P1' after Ferdinand engraved the initials 'P1' on to the chassis and other parts. It was the world's very first Porsche.

BELOW: The Egger-Lohner C.2 Phaeton was the first Porsche-designed vehicle.

ABOVE: Lohner and Porsche joined forces to produce the first hybrid vehicle, the Lohner-Porsche-Mixte.

The P1 would foreshadow Porsche's future success in motor sport when it was put through its paces in a 40km race in Berlin in September 1899. Porsche drove the P1 himself with three passengers and finished over 18 minutes clear of the field to claim victory and a gold medal, as well as winning the test for the most efficient car. It was a roaring success that only caused his stock as an engineer to rise.

Porsche soon set to work with Lohner as his new chief designer, starting the job just two months after his victory in Berlin. He soon developed an electric hub motor that would be instrumental to the design of the Lohner-Porsche car, which was revealed in 1900. It was at its presentation at the World Exhibition in Paris that Lohner claimed Porsche had a "great career ahead of him", firmly putting him on the world stage.

The Lohner-Porsche would undergo further development later that year as Porsche combined the electric wheel hub motor with a petrol engine, making the 'Lohner-Porsche Mixte' the first example of hybrid technology in a motor vehicle. The vehicles went into production in 1902.

In 1906, Porsche left Lohner to become the technical director of Austro-Daimler, where he quickly outlined his desire to produce a racing car that could win the prestigious Prinz Heinrich race, a competition for production cars in the Austro-Hungarian Empire. Porsche's first entry to the race saw

BELOW: Ferdinand Porsche continued to work with Lohner until 1906. The experience laid the foundations for a successful career.

Mercedes, the German branch of Daimler, take victory, but in 1910, Porsche-designed cars took the top three positions. And of course, Porsche himself was behind the wheel of the winning car.

Porsche's continued success came in tandem with the growth of his own family, having married Aloisia in 1903. Their first child, Louise Porsche, was born in 1904, before Ferdinand Anton Ernst Porsche, better known as Ferry Porsche, arrived five years later. On the day Ferry was born, Porsche was competing in a hill-climb race at the Semmering mountain – winning his class, naturally – and would learn of his son's birth via telegram. Both of Porsche's children would go on to play a critical role in the future of the company.

The outbreak of World War I in 1914 saw Austro-Daimler's resources divert to producing vehicles for the war effort. Porsche was tasked with transferring the engine technology from his cars to trains to assist in the war, again marking himself out as one of Europe's leading engineers and designers.

But his true passion always lay with high-performance cars and competing with them wherever possible. In 1922, Austro-Daimler produced a new four-cylinder racing car, the Sascha, named after an Austrian count who had encouraged Porsche to design a lightweight sports car. The Sascha won its class at the famous Targa Florio road race in Italy that year and was met with acclaim for its impressive speed and durability given its small size and engine. The Sascha was also sampled by 12-year-old Ferry, who was already taking after his father with a passion for cars and racing.

Porsche left Austro-Daimler in 1923 as the company struggled with financial issues, upping sticks to Stuttgart to join Daimler-Motoren-Gesellschaft. There he oversaw the design of a number of Mercedes cars, including the Mercedes Compressor sports car which won the Targa Florio outright in 1924. The success prompted Stuttgart's University of Applied

OPPOSITE:
Ferdinand's two children, Ferry and Louise, would both go on to play key roles in the future of Porsche.

BELOW: The Porsche Type 32 was an important design in what would ultimately become the 'Volkswagen'.

Sciences to award Porsche an honorary doctorate in engineering (his second, the first coming in 1917). But the name Dr. Ing. h.c. F. Porsche was about to grace much more than just his degree certificate.

On 25 April 1931, Dr. Ing. h.c. F. Porsche GmbH, a company providing services for design, engineering and consultation regarding vehicles and engines, was officially opened for business. Porsche ran his new operation out of Stuttgart along with his son-in-law, Anton Piëch, and hired a number of former colleagues, as well as drafting in Ferry to work for him.

Porsche worked on several contracts around this time, including those focused on the design of a new, everyday vehicle. It had to be affordable to both produce and for consumers to purchase; efficient, warranting a sleek, aerodynamic shape; and practical. The first Porsche design was

LEFT: Ferry Porsche (right) quickly showed the same panache as his father for design and engineering.

for Auto Union's Wanderer brand in 1931, but the designs were slowly refined across the Porsche Type 12 project, for Zündapp, before working with motorcycle company NSU on what would be known as the Porsche Type 32. NSU ultimately stopped working with Porsche as it favoured a project with Fiat. But the work that had gone into the Type 32's design would not be wasted.

ABOVE: Auto Union racing cars dominated grand prix racing in the 1930s.

While the idea of an Auto für Jedermann ('everyman's automobile') was being pursued by Porsche, it was still working hard at the other end of the automotive spectrum: high-performance race cars. In 1932, despite having no commissions, Porsche and wealthy racer Adolf Rosenberger founded Hochleistungsfahrzeugbau GmbH, literally translating as 'High Performance Car Ltd.'.

When the regulations for a new formula of Grand Prix racing in 1933 were announced, Porsche set to work on a project known as the P-Wagen that would ultimately pique the interest of Auto Union. This new company had been formed in 1932 as an amalgamation of Germany's struggling car makers and would soon gain state support under the new Nazi government led by Adolf Hitler, who took power in 1933.

Grand Prix racing had been dominated in the early 1930s by manufacturers from France and Italy, but Hitler was eager for Germany to prove its might on an automotive level, leading to state backing for its motor sport programmes through Auto Union and Mercedes to the tune of 250,000 Reichsmarks each per year. With this funding, Auto Union purchased Porsche's high performance company and the P-Wagen project, harnessing the power of a 4.4-litre, supercharged V16 engine. Known as the 'Silver Arrows' after the colours of their car, Auto Union and Mercedes would go on to dominate Grand Prix racing through the remainder of the 1930s.

Porsche played a key role in the success of Auto Union on a global stage, but there was a far bigger project that Hitler had in mind for a source of German national pride: the Volkswagen.

Porsche met with Hitler in 1934 to discuss the project, where he found the chancellor had clear ideas. He wanted the car to be affordable at under 1,000 Reichmarks, which the

BELOW: As well as tasting success on-track, Auto Union cars were built to special designs to chase land speed records.

ABOVE: The Porsche Type 12 designed by Ferdinand Porsche served as a further step towards the first Volkswagen.

everyday German worker could save up for via stamps. It had to comfortably accommodate a family and be able to cruise along the new autobahns that were being laid across the country. America had become a car-driving nation thanks to the Ford Model T; Germany would not be left behind.

The idea of a 'people's car' was not appealing to other established German automakers, but Porsche had already been working on a design for such a project through the Type 32. An impressed Hitler awarded Porsche the contract, with tests for the first prototypes beginning later in the year. Porsche also began to oversee the establishment of mass production facilities for the Volkswagen, taking inspiration from the plants he had seen during a visit to Ford's facilities in the United States.

Development and prototype testing continued apace through the late 1930s as Hitler increased his power across Europe, pushing the continent closer and closer to war. Control of the project was taken over by the German Labour Front in

1937, forming a company that would be renamed in 1938 as Volkswagenwerk, the precursor to the Volkswagen business.

In 1938, Hitler declared the car would be renamed the KdF-Wagen, standing for 'Kraft durch Freude' ('strength through joy'), which was the Nazi state's worker organisation. "It is for the broad masses that this car has been built," he said. "Its purpose is to answer their transportation needs, and it is intended to give them joy."

LEFT: The KdF-Wagen was intended to bring affordable mass mobility to the German population under the Nazis.

BELOW: The Porsche Type 64 was one of its first sports cars built to race – only for the outbreak of war to scupper plans.

Ferdinand Porsche may have been occupied with the plans for the KdF-Wagen to enter production, but he could not pull himself away from the idea of chasing performance. He wanted a mass production sports car that had appeal to the KdF as it could show Germany's prowess in competition. It led to the development of the Type 64, which became a precursor to the Porsche sports cars that would follow. The idea was to enter it into a Rome to Berlin road race, proposed as part of the alliance between Germany and Italy's dictators, only for the Sudeten Crisis of 1938 and Hitler's invasion of Poland in 1939 to prevent the race from ever going ahead. Just three Type 64s were ever built.

The KdF-Wagen was also produced in far more limited numbers than intended, when the outbreak of World War II forced the plant to shift its focus to military production. Only a few hundred KdF-Wagens were produced, all of which went

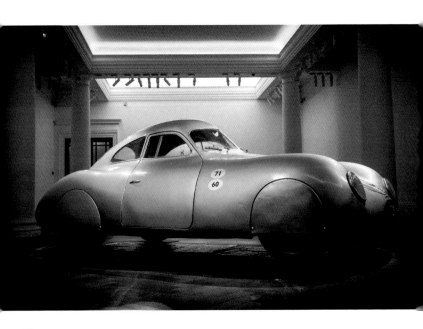

ABOVE: Ferdinand Porsche (left) shows Adolf Hitler a model prototype of the Volkswagen in 1938.

to high-ranking German officials, contrary to their original intention. As the war raged on, both Stuttgart and Wolfsburg, where the Volkswagenwerk was based, became targets for Allied bombing, prompting Porsche to relocate to the quiet town of Gmünd, Austria in 1944 so it could continue its design work in seclusion out of an old sawmill.

At the end of World War II in 1945, Ferdinand Porsche was arrested by French authorities along with his son-in-law, Anton Piëch, and Ferry, who was released after six months. With Ferdinand imprisoned for his part in Germany's war effort, it was left to Ferry to pick up the pieces as Porsche started fresh.

Ferry was able to keep the company afloat and secured a contract to design a race car, the Type 360, for Italian manufacturer Cisitalia in 1946. The funds were paid up front, part of which Ferry used to secure his father's release in 1947. They would also be the catalyst for Porsche to rise out of the ashes of war with its first production automobile: the Porsche 356.

OUT OF THE ASHES

THE ROAD TO RECOVERY

> "In the beginning I looked around, but could not find the car I was dreaming of. So I decided to build it myself."

This quote from Ferry Porsche evokes everything Porsche stands for as a car brand. As he stood looking around at the wood-panelled sawmill in Gmünd that had become Porsche's post-war headquarters, and with his father still imprisoned, to hold such grand ambition would have seemed fanciful.

But Ferry quickly set about getting Porsche back on its feet, working with his sister, Louise, to register the new company in Austria once the war had ended. The Cisitalia car project had helped bring in some much-needed financial backing, allowing Ferry to pursue the design and production of the first Porsche sports car.

"Things became tough for me after the war, since now I had to take the initiative all by myself," Ferry would later recall. But he was able to quickly find inspiration that would lead to the birth of the Porsche 356.

OPPOSITE: Ferdinand Porsche was held by French authorities for his role in Germany's war effort.

RIGHT: The Porsche 356 was the first car to bear the Porsche name, starting a long and rich history.

Having sampled a variety of cars and different concepts, Ferry settled on making a small and light yet high-powered sports car. Not wishing to totally divert from the Volkswagen which had gone through so much design and development in the late 1930s, ultimately becoming the Beetle, the Porsche 356 utilised a modified version of the Volkswagen chassis and a number of other parts, combined with a much more powerful four-cylinder engine. "Cisitalia was building a small

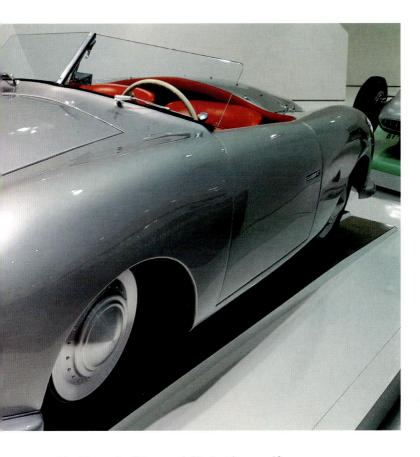

sports car with a Fiat engine," Ferry said. "So I said to myself, why shouldn't we do the same thing with VW parts? After all, that is already what we did before the war with the [Type 64] Berlin-Rome car."

On 8 June 1948, the first Porsche 356 – the Porsche 356/1, of which only one was made – was registered and rolled out of the sawmill, marking the true birth of Porsche. The No. 1 model was mid-engined and took Porsche's first competition

victory in a street race around Innsbruck in Austria, proving its credentials. The second model switched to a rear-engine layout that would ultimately carry over to the rest of the car's production.

The 356 had clear notes of both the Volkswagen Beetle and the Porsche Type 64, yet it would be the proper start of a lineage that is still evident in every single Porsche model produced today.

Across 1949, the first 52 Porsche 356s were produced by hand out of the Gmünd garage. But the humble surroundings could not last forever.

The production of the Porsche 356 came 10 months after the release of Ferdinand Porsche, who had returned to find the company in good hands with Ferry. Upon reviewing the plans for the 356 and the Cisitalia car – which would never ultimately race after its Italian backer ran out of cash – Ferdinand told those close to him he would have "done exactly the same as Ferry, right down to the last screw."

It was a ringing endorsement for Ferry, who was becoming increasingly hands-on as his father's health began to worsen. Ferdinand's passion for engineering and love for the brand he had created was being passed down to further generations. Ferry's son, Ferdinand Alexander Porsche, known as 'Butzi', was born in 1935, while Ferdinand Piëch, the son of Ferry's sister, came along two years later. Named after his grandfather, Piëch knew from an early age that he wanted to go into the family business, ultimately embarking on a degree in mechanical engineering at university.

Word soon began to spread about the quality of the Porsche 356. Sports car enthusiasts across Europe were learning of the agile, powerful nature of the car, causing demand to grow. It all meant the modest operation running out of Gmünd would simply no longer cut it. In 1950, Porsche returned to Stuttgart

OPPOSITE:
Ferdinand Porsche pictured with two of his grandchildren. Ferdinand Piëch (right) would go on to have a critical role in Porsche's future.

ABOVE: The beginnings for the 356 were humble, but it quickly became a hit that put Porsche on the map.

as it leased space in the factory of Reutter, which produced the bodies for the 356, and the orders continued to flood in.

Through the early 1950s, the United States would become one of Porsche's key markets, largely thanks to the work of Max Hoffman, an Austrian immigrant who established himself as a notable car importer in New York. At the Paris Motor Show in 1950, Hoffman met with Ferry Porsche, who said he wanted to sell five Porsche 356s per year in the United States. Hoffman replied: "If I can't sell five cars a week, I'm not interested."

It quickly led to a deal to export Porsches to the US, laying the foundations for a fruitful partnership that far exceeded Hoffman's five-per-week promise. As the 356 gained more and more interest, Hoffman made suggestions on how to modify the car to suit the American market, making it smaller and more affordable. It would lead to the Porsche 356 Speedster being released in 1954 for under $3,000, allowing it to quickly gain cult status.

Ferdinand Porsche would see the company bearing his name settle into the new Stuttgart factory and gain a foothold in the United States. But in November 1950, he suffered a stroke from which he never fully recovered, ultimately passing away in January 1951. A young boy's curiosity for electricity and engineering had established the foundations for what would become not one, but two of the world's biggest car brands in Porsche and Volkswagen, leaving an indelible mark on the automotive industry.

In 1951 Porsche would also encapsulate Ferdinand's desire to compete against the very best by entering the 24 Hours of Le Mans for the first time, after the race organisers personally invited Porsche's founding father one year earlier. The French

BELOW: Auguste Veuillet and Edmond Mouche scored class victory on Porsche's Le Mans debut in 1951, driving a 356 SL Coupe.

OVERLEAF: The Porsche 550 Spyder prototype sits in front of the New York City skyline.

ABOVE: The 1950s would mark the start of Porsche's racing escapades, hinting at great success to follow.

race was first held in 1923 and had quickly established itself as the greatest test of a sports car's endurance and reliability, not just its performance. Porsche entered a modified version of the 356, called the 356 SL Gmünd-Coupé, which took victory on debut in its class and finished 19th overall. It would mark the start of a long love affair between Porsche and the Circuit de la Sarthe.

But Porsche quickly realised that simply modifying production cars would not be enough to taste regular success on the racetrack. If it wanted to really prove itself, it would need to produce a car that was born to race, leading to the creation of the Porsche 550.

The concept behind the 550 was that you could drive the car to the track, race it, and then drive it home again.

Only 90 550s were ever made, the first three featuring a removable top before the 550 roadster – known as the 550 Spyder – became the most successful and by far the more famous version of what is regarded to be Porsche's first racing car. Its aspirations to succeed on the track were met from day one: the 550's racing debut came at the Nürburgring Eifelrennen in 1953, where Helmut Glöckler took victory on debut.

The Porsche 550 quickly replaced the 356 as the car of choice to race at Le Mans, making its debut in 1953. Its cars would finish 1-2 in the S-1500 class, putting in a dominant display that saw both 550s run ahead of those entered to the more senior classes throughout the race.

Meanwhile, Porsche's reputation in the United States was growing rapidly, quickly attracting the interest of James Dean, one of the most famous movie stars in the world. Through 1954, he became increasingly curious about becoming a racing

BELOW: James Dean gets ready to race at Palm Springs in 1955, driving a Porsche 356 Super Speedster.

driver, and after completing the filming of *East of Eden* in 1954, he purchased a Porsche 356 Super Speedster. Dean made his racing debut in a race at Palm Springs in March 1955, matching his white racing helmet to the sleek car livery with the car number, 23F, emblazoned on the side. He took victory in the novice class at the very first attempt, finishing second overall, and would also impress in races at Bakersfield and Santa Barbara. Warner Brothers soon learned of Dean's new hobby and banned him from racing in order to focus on his new film, *Giant*, through the rest of the year.

Once filming for *Giant* wrapped, Dean quickly turned his attention back to racing. He traded in his 356 Super Speedster and stumped up the cash for a 550 Spyder, having quickly learned of its racing prowess. He called the car 'Little Bastard', written in script above the rear licence plate, as well as preparing for racing by getting number 130 written on the side. Dean was ready to get back on the track now he was free of his filming duties, setting his sights on a race in Salinas in September.

But Dean's 'Little Bastard' Porsche would play a part in one of Hollywood's greatest tragedies. He was involved in some minor scrapes during the first few days of owning the car, but was still eager to race at Salinas that weekend. On 30 September 1955, when travelling to the race along Route 466, Dean collided at speed with a 1950 Ford Tudor that was turning after having no time to react. Dean was killed instantly, at the age of 24, while his passenger, Porsche mechanic Rolf Wütherich, sustained severe injuries after being thrown from the cockpit.

With sales of the 356 going strong and demand increasing after introducing the Speedster model in 1954, Porsche was able to place more and more focus on its racing efforts. The Porsche 718 was the next racing car to be produced following

OPPOSITE: Dean's Porsche 550 Spyder was known as 'Little Bastard'. The car would gain notoriety after his death in September 1955.

ABOVE: The Porsche 718 became a force throughout the major sports car races around the world.

development of the 550, sticking with the mid-engined layout that had proved so successful. The car's full name was the 718 RSK, RS standing for 'Renn Sport' ('sports racing') and the 'K' for the shape of the torsion bars at the rear, again signalling its primary purpose was for the racetrack.

The Porsche 718 debuted at Le Mans in 1957, and soon fought for top honours in many of the world's biggest sports

car races. Jean Behra and Hans Herrmann finished third overall at Le Mans in 1958, and one year later, Edgar Barth and Wolfgang Seidel claimed Porsche's maiden overall win at the Targa Florio in Italy.

Formula 1 had also emerged on Porsche's radar. Its debut came at the German Grand Prix in 1957, when Barth and Umberto Maglioli raced a pair of 550s before the 718 RSK

BELOW: Dan Gurney scored Porsche's sole factory Formula 1 victory at the 1962 French Grand Prix.

OPPOSITE: The Porsche 904 proved impressive both on the track and on the road.

finished sixth at the Nürburgring one year later. In 1959, Porsche adjusted the design of the 718 to give it a narrower body that was more familiar and successful among formula cars, before ultimately embarking on its first full F1 season in 1961. Dan Gurney scored three second-place finishes, but would have to wait until the arrival of the Porsche 804 – a single-seater, bespoke racing car designed by Butzi Porsche – before finally winning a race.

Gurney's breakthrough came in the 1962 French Grand Prix at Rouen, where he finished a lap ahead of the field to give Porsche what would be its only F1 victory. The Porsche 804 only raced eight times before the plug was pulled on the F1 programme in favour of focusing on sports car racing and to save costs. The Porsche 904 sports car was launched in 1964, again designed by Butzi Porsche, whose abilities were becoming more and more revered within the company. A

street-legal version of the 904 was required to comply with the regulations to race, the demand for which far outstripped supply.

Through all of Porsche's racing escapades, the 356 had been ticking along as the backbone of the company. In 1958, one decade after the first model had rolled out of the sawmill in Gmünd, the 10,000th Porsche 356 came off the production line. It was a landmark moment for Porsche. The acquisition of Reutter, the body contractor out of whose factory it had operated for a while, was another sign of Porsche's growth into a self-sufficient, ambitious car manufacturer.

Attention was quickly turning to the 356's successor and what the future may hold. Just as Ferry had played a key role in the success of the first production Porsche under the stewardship of his father, his own son, Butzi, was about to play his part in the birth of one of the most legendary cars in automotive history.

LEFT: Ferry Porsche (left) with his son, Ferdinand Alexander – known as Butzi – inspecting the rear of a Porsche 356.

THE BIRTH OF A
LEGEND

THE 911 REVOLUTION

> Success on the track and booming sales across the world gave Porsche all the incentive it needed to take another step with its car designs, pursuing something bigger, more powerful and more ambitious.

The Porsche 911 would go on to become one of the most instantly recognisable sports cars in automotive history, as well as enjoying a longevity most models could only dream to achieve. Designed as a replacement for the Porsche 356, plans were formulated in the early 1960s. Ferdinand Alexander Porsche, known as Butzi, was in charge of the styling department around this time, and after playing a key role in the design of the 904, he was eager to get involved with his father's new focus, the 911.

Butzi set to work on a fresh concept for a car that would take over as the brand's flagship model, formulating blueprints for what would be known as the Porsche Typ 754 T7. The task of keeping the car small and light enough to retain Porsche's famed agility while fitting it with a bigger engine proved difficult, but the T7

OPPOSITE: Three generations of Porsche: Ferdinand, Ferry and Ferdinand Alexander. The family nature of the business would later become a point of contention.

ABOVE: The Porsche Type 754 T7 would lay the foundations for the birth of the 911 legend.

would be the forefather for what would ultimately become the Porsche 911, with its iconic flat nose and bulging headlights.

The initial T7 design featured two rear seats and a raised roof to give headroom for those sitting in the back, but Ferry Porsche insisted on a coupé design for the new car. Initially, Butzi's father was totally against the idea of having four seats in the car, but recognised the need for practicality and agreed to the 2+2 design, retaining the sloping rear. It would be the final major adjustment that led to the iconic shape the 911 would come to bear.

The 911 was never meant to be called the 911. When production commenced on the new car that would succeed the 356, it was known as the Porsche 901. The car was revealed at the Frankfurt Motor Show in September 1963, featuring a new two-litre, 130 bhp engine and a five-speed gearbox which could help reach a top speed of 130 mph and do 0-60 in 8.3 seconds. It was a big statement to the world that truly marked the 911 out as the next generation of Porsche cars.

Production started one year later, only for Porsche to quickly face opposition when it presented the car in Paris in October 1964. A delegation from Peugeot informed Porsche officials that only they had the rights to sell cars in France named with three-digit numbers that used a 0 in the middle. While this only impacted Porsche in one country, it opted to make the change and rename the 901 the 911. The 904 also had to be renamed the Porsche Carrera GTS.

BELOW: Pressure from Peugeot over the naming designation meant the Porsche 901 became the 911.

THE BIRTH OF A LEGEND 51

ABOVE: With its iconic sloping rear, the Porsche 911 was an instant classic.

Production of the Porsche 911 began in earnest in late 1964 after being rechristened – although a handful of cars badged as 901s were produced – and it quickly became a hit among those who had become enamoured with the German manufacturer's push for high performance. Although it was undeniably an evolution from the 356, the 911 marked a big leap forward in every regard, from its exterior and bodywork to its plush interior.

The design of the car had all been overseen by Butzi, who at the age of 28 had etched his name into an important part of Porsche's history. He would later reflect how his immersion within the family company under the wing of his father, Ferry, during regular visits to the Porsche factory as a boy had led

him to take such a keen interest in car design and development. "I was proud and happy to be a part of all this," he said. "I imagine that some of the hours I spent [at the factory as a child] must have lingered in my mind." Butzi was not the only descendant of Ferdinand Porsche to have become part of the family business. His cousin, Ferdinand Piëch, had graduated from university in 1962 after writing a thesis on an F1 engine and would join Porsche the following year, focusing on its motor sport affairs.

Although the Porsche 911 had not abandoned the goal to ensure its design was compact, ensuring the power of the engine was not bogged down, the new car was more practical in many ways than the 356. The wheelbase had been extended

ABOVE: The interior of the 911 made the car as beautiful on the inside as it was on the outside.

OPPOSITE: The Porsche 912 was a success thanks to its lower price compared to the 911.

by 10 centimetres, making the cockpit slightly bigger, while the suspension layout was redesigned to ensure there was more luggage space.

But that did not mean it was an entirely perfect entry-level sports car. The added power of the engine, while suiting thrill-chasing enthusiasts with deep pockets, meant the Porsche 911 had become out of reach for many. It forced Porsche into a rethink, particular with the 356 on its way out as its primary production model.

The result was the Porsche 912, which became the new entry-level Porsche in 1965. By fitting the four-cylinder engine that had powered the 356 into the body of the 911, it managed to cater for those with a more modest budget, bringing the cost of the car down by around a quarter. The Porsche 912 proved so popular that it initially outsold the 911.

ABOVE: Porsches were becoming more and more of a fashion symbol.

With the 912 now on the market, production of the 356 finally came to an end in 1966. Sales of the car had remained strong well into the 1960s, particularly in the United States, where many still favoured it over the larger 911, while the final run of Porsche 356 C models had more powerful engines and disc brakes. The last 10 models were supplied to the Dutch police force, leaving the final tally of Porsche 356s produced at

77,361. Ferry Porsche believed back in 1948 that he would only be able to sell 500. To this day, it is believed around half of the Porsche 356s produced remain in existence, the majority of which can be found in the United States – a lasting sign of how the car became such a cult vehicle in the American market.

The success of the 911 and 912 prompted Porsche to keep working on the development of the model and refine it

BELOW: The 911 Targa's roll hoop stayed in place to comply with US safety laws.

further. This led to the unveiling of the Porsche 911S in 1966, which looked to take a step forward for the car's outright performance. On the outside, the car looked very similar to the standard 911; under the bonnet, it was a very different story. The screaming, more powerful engine provided an added thrill on top of the agility and nimbleness Porsches had built their reputation upon.

The 911S was complemented by the Porsche 911 Targa, named after the famed Targa Florio race in Italy. Porsche had been trying to find a way to make an open-top version of its famed sports car, yet there were calls in the United States for them to be outlawed completed on safety grounds. Porsche found a way to satisfy the requirements with the Targa: the full roll hoop remained in place at all times, but the roof and rear window could be folded down, making it possible for an open-

air experience. The car launched in 1967 and would set the tone for future models to come with this new concept.

But upon seeing the 911S push the performance of its new flagship car and begin to fare well in competition, winning in class at Le Mans in 1966, Porsche began to mull how it could take another step forward. The first plans were put together the same year for a new edition of the car, the Porsche 911R, which would be overseen by Porsche's new motor sport R&D chief: Ferdinand Piëch.

Piëch had been making a name for himself on the motor sport side of the company that bore his grandfather's surname, leading to his move into a new role. The aim for the 911R – R standing for 'Renn', German for 'race' – was to provide an improved power-to-weight ratio. The target was for the car to weigh 800kg and deliver 210 bhp, equalling less than 4kg per

BELOW: The Porsche 911R – R standing for '*Renn*' or 'race' – was born for the track.

bhp, which was 1.5kg less than Porsche's rivals in GT racing. The 911 was stripped out to bring the weight down, reducing the number of dials, removing the soundproofing and heaters, and even the lid of the glovebox. Fibreglass was used for much of the bodywork to bring the weight down further.

The car was over 200kg lighter than the 911S, but also almost twice the price at 45,000 Deutschmarks, making it difficult to sell to consumers. The focus for the 911R became on its racing escapades, which included a remarkable performance in an 84-hour race at the Nürburgring in 1967, where Vic Elford, Hans Herrmann and Jochen Neerpasch completed over 1,000km more than any other entrant.

Piëch's focus on competition had one primary goal at its heart: outright victory at the 24 Hours of Le Mans. Ford and Ferrari dominated the race through the 1960s, enjoying a heated rivalry, but Porsche had rarely been vying in the top class. Yet it was becoming more and more clear that success at Le Mans was not only about sporting pride – it was also a huge marketing tool. The idea of a car that was both quick and reliable, outlasting the opposition for 24 hours in the most notable race in the world, would be huge.

Overseeing the motor sport department at Porsche, Piëch took a similar approach in designing the new Porsche 906 car as he did with the 911R, focusing chiefly on weight reduction from the 904 that his cousin Butzi had helped design.

The 906 debuted in 1966 at the Daytona 24 Hours and went on to dominate its class at Le Mans, as well as filling out the places from fourth to seventh overall, only trailing the more powerful Ford GT40s in the premier class. Piëch's team continued to develop and adjust the 906, moving the driver position from the left to the right of the cockpit for the 907 in a bid to offer better sightlines for clockwise tracks, but the more powerful Fords and Ferraris remained out of reach.

ABOVE: Vic Elford drives the Porsche 911T to victory at the 1968 Rallye Monte Carlo.

Change was afoot at the top of global sports car racing. Ahead of the 1968 season, motor sport's global governing body, the FIA, announced a 3-litre engine limit for prototypes racing in the top class in a bid to reduce speeds. It was a big blow to Ford and Ferrari, with the latter cancelling its prototype programme altogether as a result, but it meant Porsche could compete at the highest level for the first time. The Porsche 908 still couldn't grab that elusive win at Le Mans, despite taking pole position with Jo Siffert. Piëch's hunger for glory at La Sarthe remained strong.

Porsche tasted success elsewhere in motor sport. In 1968, a Porsche 911T – the new entry-level version of the 911 – won the Monte Carlo Rally for the first time before the 911S scored wins in each of the two years that followed. Vic Elford, Porsche's first Monte winner, called it "the best car I have ever driven in my life". Elford would go on to win the Daytona 24

BELOW: The Porsche 914 was a result of collaboration with Volkswagen, meeting the needs of both manufacturers.

OPPOSITE: Ferry Porsche poses on the bonnet of a Porsche 911 in 1968.

Hours just one week later in a Porsche 907, before taking the win at the Targa Florio with a new lap record, making 1968 a very successful year for both him and Porsche.

The introduction of the 911T at a cheaper price point spoke to the need for Porsche to cater to buyers with more modest budgets. The 912 had served as the base-level car for much of the decade, but when Volkswagen found itself in need of a new top-end model, Porsche saw a chance to work together once again. The result was the six-cylinder Porsche 914, the four-cylinder version of which was sold as a Volkswagen.
The mid-engined car looked markedly different to the 911, sporting a long wheelbase, but quickly became a hit upon its release in 1969.

Yet nothing could take the shine away from the 911, which had surged to become one of the most popular and coveted sports cars in the world, and remains so to this day. It only furthered Porsche's reputation as a world leader in the automotive sphere – yet it still needed to make that same statement on the track after so many near misses at Le Mans. As the 1970s beckoned, all of that was about to change in emphatic fashion.

GLORY AND
GROWING PAINS

VICTORY AT LAST

> Ferdinand Piëch was not a man who did things by halves. After taking the helm of Porsche's motor sport affairs and getting it so close to victory at Le Mans towards the end of the 1960s, he remained determined to take another huge step forward and finally secure the crown he so coveted.

While the decision to limit prototypes to 3-litre engines had helped bring Porsche into contention for outright victory at Le Mans, the backlash from manufacturers meant there was little interest to pursue the class properly. To remedy this, officials announced in April 1968 that 5-litre Group 4 sports cars would be eligible to race, and that only 25 units had to be built, down from the 50 previously required.

It spurred Porsche to leap at the opportunity to design a brand new racing car that would be known as the Porsche 917. The project was signed off over the summer of 1968, and by spring 1969, the car was ready to be unveiled at the Geneva Motor Show

OPPOSITE: In 1970, the 917K would score the first of Porsche's 19 outright victories at the 24 Hours of Le Mans.

OPPOSITE: Steve McQueen's famous movie *Le Mans* had Porsche's success central to its story.

– retail price 140,000 Deutschmarks – ahead of its Le Mans debut a few months later. Piëch made a punchy statement to racing officials by having a long line of all 25 Porsche 917s required arranged outside the Zuffenhausen factory.

Yet the 917 initially proved very difficult to handle, meaning its early racing efforts were far from successful through 1969. At Le Mans, privateer driver John Woolfe died in a crash on the opening lap of the race, leading to the end of the traditional start that saw drivers run to their cars before pulling away, often without their doors or seat belts fully attached.

The 917 was undeniably quick, though, meaning that once Piëch's team had fixed the troublesome handling and cured its reliability woes, it finally lived up to the hype. Nine 917s took the start at Le Mans in 1970, going up against a gaggle of competitive Ferrari 512s, but Porsche finally got its breakthrough victory. The 917 dominated a race of attrition in which many drivers struggled in wet conditions, taking a 1-2 finish as Hans Hermann and Richard Attwood scored Porsche's first outright victory at Le Mans.

It was also in 1970 that Hollywood came to the French classic as Steve McQueen filmed his famous movie, *Le Mans*, using the event as the backdrop. McQueen was meant to enter the race alongside F1 world champion Jackie Stewart, only for his insurance company to refuse to cover him for an event in France. But that didn't stop *Le Mans* from making the Porsche 917 a cult icon when the film was released in 1971. After crashing out of the race, McQueen's character, Michael Delaney, is asked by his team manager to take over in another 917 to complete the race, saying: "Michael, I want you to drive flat out. I want Porsche to win Le Mans." Delaney duly obliges, helping Porsche to win, just as in reality, with a 1-2 finish. Filming took place during the race at Le Mans as cameras were fitted to a Porsche 908 that was entered, while the

track was then hired out for three months after the race to get further shots. Naturally, McQueen did most of his own stunts throughout filming.

As well as gaining recognition on the big screen, the Porsche 917 also emerged as the most dominant sports car in the motor sport through the early 1970s. A second outright Le Mans win followed in 1971 with Gijs van Lennep and Helmut Marko, who combined to set a distance record of 3,315 miles that stood until 2010, aided by a radical magnesium frame. A modified version of the car, known as the 917/20, ran in a famed 'pink pig' livery that had cuts of meat written across the chassis. While it failed to finish, it was an important test bed for Porsche as it looked across the Atlantic for further success with the 917.

From 1972, the rules at Le Mans were changed again to cut speeds and reduce engine output, prompting the 908 to become Porsche's car of choice. But the Can-Am sports

OPPOSITE: Porsche won Le Mans again in 1971 as Helmut Marko and Gijs van Lennep set a distance record that stood until 2010.

BELOW: Porsche's 'pink pig' livery, seen here on the 917/20 model, would become iconic throughout motorsport.

GLORY AND GROWING PAINS 71

car series in North America still favoured the high-powered engines, giving the 917 a new lease of life. Piëch was keen to keep pushing the boundaries of performance, prompting Porsche to explore a number of different routes for its engine in Can-Am, where there were open rules. Porsche opted to go down the force induction route, creating a turbocharged five-litre flat-12 engine with an output of more than 900 bhp in the 917/10. George Follmer dominated the championship, scoring five wins in nine races after Mark Donohue, who had been integral to the development of the engine, was forced to miss much of the season following a testing crash.

Donohue would sweep to the championship in 1973 after Porsche refined the 917 further, resulting in the 917/30 that broke the 1,000 bhp barrier. The longer wheelbase cured some

of the stability issues with the 917/10. Donohue won six races in Can-Am, the remaining two also being won by Porsche factory drivers, and commented that the 917/30 was "the only car I've ever driven that can spin the tyres at 200 mph".

All good things have to come to an end, and the same was true of the 917. The global fuel crisis combined with dissatisfaction over Porsche's domination prompted Can-Am officials to bring in new fuel limits starting in 1974. It marked the end of Porsche's foray in the series, but it remained eager to give the 917 one final hurrah. In 1975, the 917/30 came out of retirement to set a closed circuit land speed record at Talladega Speedway in the United States as Donohue reached 221.1mph – the ultimate showing of what Porsche was capable of on the racetrack.

BELOW: After rules at Le Mans changed, the Porsche 917 crossed the ocean and dominated the Can-Am Series in North America.

ABOVE: The Porsche 911 was proving successful on-track too, winning the Daytona 24 Hours on its debut in 1973.

Porsche's flagship road car, the Porsche 911, was also enjoying success on the track. The Porsche 911 RSR Carrera was developed as part of Porsche's push to try and regain supremacy in sports car racing after focusing much of its efforts on the 917 prototype. It was the first time the 911 had been given a dedicated racing effort, leading to its debut at the 24 Hours of Daytona in February 1973. Two factory cars were entered, but had to be entered in the prototype class as they had not completed the FIA's homologation process. It didn't stop Peter Gregg and Hurley Haywood from taking a dominant win.

All of the experience Porsche had gained with tuning the engine for the 917 prompted it to explore options for the 911 in racing settings, paving the way for the first Porsche 911 RSR Carrera Turbo. The car finished second overall at Le Mans in

1974, and while it would have a short racing life, as Porsche turned attention to the new Group 5 regulations and the development of the 935, the requirement for production models meant a road-going turbocharged 911 was on the horizon.

The Porsche 911 Turbo, known as the Porsche 930 in North America, went into production in 1975 and quickly became a hit. The 3-litre engine produced 260 bhp and had distinctive flared wings on the rear spoiler, but retained the short wheelbase the 911 was known for, offering another huge step forward for the most recognisable car from the 'House of Porsche'.

And yet by the mid-1970s, fractures had emerged within the family that meant it wasn't truly the House of Porsche any more. The rapid growth of the company meant the scale was too big for it to remain a true family business. By now it was all a far cry from the Gmünd sawmill from where Ferry Porsche had lifted his father's company out of the ashes of war and revived its fortunes.

BELOW: Ferry Porsche and race director Rico Steinemann watch on at Le Mans.

ABOVE: The Porsche 924 was designed to be the new entry-level car in its range, replacing the 912.

The expansion of the various racing escapades and their associated costs had taken a toll on Porsche by the early 1970s. Ferry Porsche had concerns of what may become of the company should it not take action, favouring a shift towards becoming a public limited company. Piëch, who had been so integral to so much of its motor sport success, was diametrically opposed to his uncle's view on this, and had backing from his mother Louise (Ferry's sister) in wanting it to very much remain a family-run operation.

It all led to a family summit at Zell am See, where Ferdinand Porsche had moved to in 1941 and the family residence had remained ever since. There it was agreed that Porsche would become a public limited company, Porsche AG – and crucially, there would be no prominent family members

on the executive board, including Ferry, who had learned of the concept from Honda in Japan. But Ferry was appointed chairman of the supervisory board, meaning he retained a significant sway over the company. Piëch was furious at how the other side of his family had acted, claiming: "You are domestic pigs. I'm the wild boar." He would soon end up at Audi, while cousin Butzi would establish his own firm, Porsche Design.

As Porsche's new management set-up settled in, attention turned to replacing the 912 as the entry-level car, given the 911 was still going strong and catering at the higher end of its range. The result was the Porsche 924, a front-engined sports coupé that was rear wheel drive, making it the first car out of Porsche in this configuration, as well as being the marque's first

BELOW: The famous Porsche 935/78, better known as 'Moby Dick' for its long tail design.

water-cooled model. Like the 912, the 924 was intended to be a joint venture between Porsche and Volkswagen, only for VW to pull out and focus on models lower down its range. Porsche opted to buy the design rights back from VW, leading to the 924 being launched in 1976, although it was fitted with an Audi engine. It nevertheless quickly won acclaim for its sleek design, including pop-up headlights, and comparatively low price compared to the 911.

Porsche was still enjoying success on the track as the 924 hit the market. The Porsche 936 won Le Mans and the World Sportscar Championship in 1976, leading to a special Martini edition – named after the iconic livery the car bedecked in the vermouth company's colours – of the Porsche 924 being released the following year. Jacky Ickx would take back-to-back wins for Porsche at Le Mans in the 936, tasting success again in 1977, while the Porsche 935 also dominated the Group 5 regulations. The famous 'Moby Dick' Porsche 935/78 – named as such due to its long tail – was designed solely for Le Mans

ABOVE: A decade after its first win, the Porsche 911 was still going strong in the Monte Carlo Rally.

and reached 227 mph on the Hunaudières Straight in 1978, only for engine issues to prevent it from fighting at the front in the race. In the same year, the Porsche 911 Carrera also won the Monte Carlo Rally, 10 years on from the car's first win at the historic event, proving its enduring capabilities.

But the winds of change had been blowing since the power struggle resulted in a shift at the very top of Porsche. After the company went public, Ernst Fuhrmann had been appointed chairman and was quick to put pressure on Ferry Porsche to bring in a replacement for the 911. Development got under way in 1974 on a new flagship model, starting with a blank sheet of paper – unlike previous models, this would not be an evolution or adaptation of something that already existed.

The result was the Porsche 928, which was unveiled at the Geneva Motor Show in 1977 before going on sale the following year. It was the first V8-powered Porsche, immediately

BELOW: Ferdinand Piëch (far right), among the recipients of Germany's prestigious Golden Steering Wheel award in 1978.

OPPOSITE: Porsche displays its range and own commitment to perfectioh in an advert from *Motor Sport Magazine* in 1978.

cementing itself as a top-of-the-line model thanks to an eye-catching design that seemed more futuristic than the 911 it was intended to replace.

There was life in the old legend yet, though. The high price point for the 928 and the decision to pursue a front-engined, water-cooled concept – similar to the 924 – meant it did little for Porsche's core consumer base, who remained attached to the 911. Fuhrmann's successor as chairman, Peter Schutz, maintained the two cars should be sold side by side, having seen the 911 Turbo continue to sell strongly and the new 911 SC be launched in 1978.

While the 1970s had been a period of some growing pains for Porsche, its core models remained incredibly popular, and it had finally achieved the sporting breakthroughs it so craved. But it was merely a taste of what was to come in the decade to follow.

80 GLORY AND GROWING PAINS

Some people are never satisfied.

Porsche, for instance.

They couldn't simply be content with creating the most enduring and beloved sports car the world has ever known. The Porsche 911.

They had to keep on improving it. Refining its power, flexibility, reliability and roadholding. And adding even more luxury.

Did that satisfy them? Hardly. Because their attention next turned to the incredible potential of turbocharging.

And so was born the Porsche Turbo, the ultimate performance roadcar. A car which has drained motoring journalists dry of superlatives.

Now were Porsche satisfied?

Not yet. The designers, engineers and technicians of Porsche's research centre at Weissach were, in fact, already busy with Projects 928 and 924.

Two very different versions of the Porsche ideal. Front mounted, water cooled engines and sleek, new shapes.

First off the mark was the 2 litre 924 bringing Porsche motoring within reach of many more people.

Next came the car voted Car of the Year 1978, the 4.5 litre 928 V-8 luxury sports coupé. Said to be the car by which others will be judged for the next decade.

924, 911SC, 928, Turbo. Whichever you choose, Porsche believe you'll be well satisfied.

As for Porsche themselves: they will never be satisfied.

Porsche Cars Great Britain Limited, Richfield Avenue, Reading, RG1 8PH. Tel: 0734 595411.

For Tourist, NATO, Diplomatic and Personal Export Enquiries. Tel: 01-568 1313. The present Porsche line-up includes the 924 Coupe and Lux Coupe – from £8,200, the 911SC and 911SC Sport Coupe and Targa – from £13,850; the Car of the Year 1978, the 928, at £19,500 and the Turbo at £25,000. Prices shown are correct at time of going to press and include car tax, VAT and seat belts. Delivery and number plates are extra. For further information and details of leasing facilities available contact your nearest official Porsche Centre.

Main dealers: South East: A.F.N. Ltd, Isleworth. Tel: 01-560 1011. A.F.N. Ltd, Guildford. Tel: 0483 38448. Charles Follett Ltd, Mayfair. Tel: 01-629 6266. Malaya Garage (Billingshurst) Ltd, Billingshurst. Tel: 0403 81 3341. Maltin Car Concessionaires Ltd, Henley-on-Thames. Tel: 04912 4952. Motortune Ltd, Kensington. Tel: 01-581 1234. **South West:** Dick Lovett (Specialist Cars) Ltd, Wroughton. Tel: 0793 812387. **South:** Heddell and Deeks (Motors) Ltd, Bournemouth. Tel: 0202 510252. **Midlands:** Swinford Motors (Continental) Ltd, Stourbridge. Tel: 038 482 3047. Roger Clark (Cars) Ltd, Narborough. Tel: 0533 848270. Gordon Lamb Ltd, Chesterfield. Tel: 0246 451611. **East Anglia and Essex:** Lancaster Garages (Colchester) Ltd, Colchester. Tel: 0206 48141. **North West:** Ian Anthony Sales (Knutsford) Ltd. Tel: 0565 52737. **North East:** JCT 600 Ltd, Yeadon. Tel: 0532 502231. **North:** Parker and Parker Ltd, Kendal. Tel: 0539 24331. Gordon Ramsay Ltd, Newcastle upon Tyne. Tel: 0632 812828/814383. Gordon Ramsay Ltd, Bishop Auckland. Tel: 0388 5601. **Scotland:** Glen Henderson Motors Ltd, Ayr. Tel: 0292 81531. Glen Henderson Motors Ltd, Glasgow. Tel: 041-943 1155. Glen Henderson Motors Ltd, Edinburgh. Tel: 031-225 9266. **Northern Ireland:** Isaac Agnew Ltd (Retail), Glengormley. Tel: 02313 7111. Isaac Agnew Ltd, Belfast. Tel: 0232 663231. **Channel Islands:** Jones Garage, St. Saviour, Jersey. Tel: 0534 26156.

KING OF THE
TRACK

ON TOP OF THE WORLD

Porsche had seen through the 1970s just what it would be capable of achieving on the racetrack, spearheaded by the 917 programme that had really pushed the boundaries of performance.

Yet the 1980s would bring unprecedented and to this day unmatched success for Porsche across the world, dominating not only the sports car scene, but also Formula 1.

As the new decade began, the 936 remained at the forefront of sports car racing. Jacky Ickx became the first driver to score five overall victories at the 24 Hours of Le Mans in 1981, partnering Derek Bell in a 936/81 to mark the end of the Group 6 era in style. The FIA was looking to draw manufacturers away from focusing so much on engine development and to instead create more variety, leading to new limits on fuel consumption under the Group C regulations introduced for 1982.

Porsche commenced work on its new prototype, the Porsche 956, in the summer of 1981 to prepare for the incoming

OPPOSITE: Porsche started the 1980s in style as the 936 took victory at Le Mans, setting the tone for a decorated decade.

regulations, relishing the opportunity to produce a brand new model. Porsche engineers sought innovation through concepts such as the Porsche Doppelkupplung (PDK) dual-clutch transmission, which would later be a staple for its road cars, while the 2.6-litre turbo engine led to an output of over 620 bhp.

The true magic of the Porsche 956 came in its aerodynamics. The gullwing doors and slanting nose made it easy on the eye, but it was underneath the car that it was truly special. The 956 was the first Porsche to utilise ground effect – generating downforce via aerodynamic tunnels on the floor – that meant it could reach previously unmatched speeds, particularly through high-speed corners as the car stuck to the ground. Porsche claimed that per the theory of downforce, the car could drive upside down at a speed of 199.7mph – not that this point was ever possible to prove…

Ickx took his sixth and final Le Mans victory with Porsche in 1982, again alongside Bell, as the 956 swept the top three positions (followed by a pair of 935s for good measure). But that was nothing compared to Porsche's dominance one year later, when the top eight positions were all taken by Porsche 956s. The only interloper in the top 10 was a Sauber C7 that finished ninth, leading to the famous 'Nobody's Perfect' poster – a perfect display of just how powerful success at Le Mans was as a marketing tool. In 1983, Stefan Bellof set the competitive lap record on the Nürburgring's fearsome Nordschleife circuit in a Porsche 956. His lap of 6m 11.13s remains unbeaten to this day.

The regulations in place at the time meant the 956 wasn't eligible to race in the American IMSA championship, prompting Porsche into a rethink when it came to designing a successor. The result was the Porsche 962, which had a longer wheelbase and did away with the twin-turbo used on the 956.

The 962 would win twice at Le Mans, in 1986 and 1987, as well as setting a lap record in qualifying for the 1985 race as Hans-Joachim Stuck – whose father, Hans, was involved with Ferdinand Porsche's Grand Prix project in the 1930s – posted an average speed of 156.5mph. It would take 32 years for that to be beaten. Porsche scored seven wins at Le Mans in the 1980s with three different cars, yet it still had new ground to break in motor sport with success in Formula 1.

F1 teams were becoming increasingly reliant on turbo technology to be competitive, making Porsche an attractive partner given its success in the field. McLaren looked to strike a deal with Porsche, but the German manufacturer was uncertain about the significant costs involved in developing an F1 engine. McLaren boss Ron Dennis agreed to fund the early

BELOW: To this day, the Porsche 956 holds the official competitive lap record at the Nordschleife, courtesy of Stefan Bellof in 1983.

ABOVE: Porsche joined forces with TAG to create a V6 turbo engine that would go on to dominate in Formula 1 with McLaren.

phase of the programme, allowing Porsche engine guru Hans Mezger and McLaren designer John Barnard to set to work together on the new engine, which would initially be tested in a Porsche 956 chassis. Dennis managed to secure funding and technical support from Techniques d'Avant Garde for the programme, meaning the 1.5-litre V6 turbo would be badged as a TAG-Porsche.

Although testing of the engine only started in the spring of 1983, McLaren driver Niki Lauda was adamant it should be raced as soon as possible amid his dissatisfaction with the normally aspirated Ford Cosworth engine, going behind the team's back and getting sponsor Marlboro to put pressure on for a new car to be designed that would accommodate the TAG-Porsche design. Lauda ultimately got his way, meaning the engine was used for the last three races of the 1983 season, giving him a chance to iron out any issues before gunning for the championship the following year.

The TAG-Porsche engine proved to be the class of the field in 1984. It was lighter than the units from rivals Ferrari and Renault. But crucially, Porsche's renowned efficiency made it hard to beat in the races. While Lauda and team-mate Alain Prost would only score two pole positions all season, they combined for 12 race wins, proving that over a distance, nothing got close to the TAG-Porsche.

It set up a tense championship fight between Lauda and young team-mate Prost, who had joined McLaren for 1984 and made an early statement by winning on debut in Brazil. The title fight raged throughout the season and went to the wire in Portugal, where Lauda produced what he would later regard as the greatest race of his life by charging from 11th on the grid to finish second. It was enough to give him a third world

BELOW: Niki Lauda and Alain Prost were team-mates and title rivals at McLaren in 1984 as the McLaren-TAG/Porsche car proved unstoppable.

championship by half a point, while Porsche power had secured both the drivers' and constructors' championships.

Further titles would follow in 1985 and 1986 with Prost before the McLaren-TAG/Porsche project enjoyed a swansong year in 1987, by which point the Honda turbo had become the engine to beat. TAG ended its funding of the engine project, meaning Porsche's F1 foray did too. But it had been an enormously successful period, yielding 25 wins, three drivers' titles and two constructors' championships in four seasons. By the end of 1987, the engine was producing over 1,000 bhp.

Porsche also dipped its toe in IndyCar around this time. While the brand remained as strong as ever in North America, and was faring well in the IMSA SportsCar Championship, it hadn't taken a real shot at the legendary Indianapolis 500. A plan was put together for 1987 to race with a full factory

programme in the final couple of races, only for the chassis to prove disastrous, prompting Porsche to follow the other manufacturers and get a custom chassis from March. Teo Fabi was signed to drive the car and enjoyed decent success with Porsche's V8 engine, scoring victory at Mid-Ohio in 1989.

But it would prove to be Porsche's sole IndyCar victory as a push to design its own chassis collapsed when officials ruled the all-carbon fibre design could not be used. Porsche pulled the plug on IndyCar at the end of the year, instead turning its attention to an F1 engine project with Footwork for 1991, only for that to be a disaster. The engine was too heavy and was beset by continued issues, prompting Footwork to cut ties mid-season.

While Porsche's on-track fortunes took a bit of a dip towards the end of a decade that brought enormous success,

BELOW: A less successful motorsport project for Porsche came in IndyCar, recording just a single race win.

the production models had continued to fare strongly. In 1982, Porsche introduced the 944, a mid-range model that was intended to serve as a replacement for the 924. Sales for the car had dipped, prompting chairman Peter Schutz – whose decision to keep the 911 in production had paid off handsomely – to push for the 944.

The Porsche 944 was based on the 924, retaining the front-engine design, but had a revised body including flared wheel arches. It was designed as a mid-range model between the 924 and the 911 SC, and was intended to go a long way to dispelling purists' beliefs that front-engined cars weren't 'real' Porsches – a criticism not aided by the fact that the 924's engine had been designed by Audi. After teasing the car with a prototype design that raced as a GTP car at Le Mans in 1981, the new car was unveiled at the Frankfurt Motor Show later that year, promising a faster and more comfortable ride than the 924.

The 944 proved an immediate hit, helping further Porsche's expansion. A new headquarters was set up in the United States, with Porsche North America operating out of Reno, Nevada. Porsche AG also went public, offering half of all available shares to investors, with the other half being retained by the Porsche and Piëch families.

Porsche's on-track success through the 1980s was not enough to satiate finding even greater performance with its road cars. Schutz remained content with how the 911 was performing both commercially and technically against its rivals, yet there remained an eagerness to take it further.

The result was the Porsche 959, a true supercar that was all about pioneering technology and optimum performance. The 959 utilised the flat-six engine used in the 911, proving the adaptability of Porsche's most iconic model, but was capable of more than 450 bhp thanks to a twin-turbo design

OPPOSITE: Porsche's 944 was an immediate hit with consumers, and featured a jazzy interior design.

ABOVE: Porsche also proved its endurance in the fearsome Dakar Rally, scoring two outright wins.

OPPOSITE: The Porsche 959 was a true supercar that pushed the boundaries of road performance as far as possible.

and improved inter cooling. The all-wheel drive system – seen on a high-performance sports car for the first time – and striking aerodynamic design made the 959 seem futuristic. It had originally been designed to comply with the Group B rally regulations, and earned its racing stripes by winning the fearsome Dakar Rally in 1986, three years after the 953, a modified racing variant of the 911, had achieved victory.

It would not be until 1987 that consumers got the chance to buy the Porsche 959 after a series of delays. The price tag of $225,000 was eye-watering and only 292 were made, but it was a game-changer. Not only did it serve as a huge step forward for supercars; it also proved the trusty 911 remained a super base for Porsche to keep working from moving forward.

The 1980s had seen the 911 continue to sell strongly, largely thanks to the 3.2-litre Porsche 911 Carrera that was released in 1984. It was the most powerful and most beautiful version of the 911 to date, tapping into the growing affluence of the 'baby boomers'. By the end of the decade, more than 70,000 cars had been sold, and it was a firm fixture in pop culture. For the new spy series *MacGyver*, which debuted in 1985, the title character had a Porsche 911, while two variants of the 911 had featured in *Knight Rider* through the early 1980s.

OVERLEAF: Through all the on-track success and exploration of new models, nothing could quite match the charm of the classic 911.

In 1987, production of the Porsche 911 surpassed the 250,000 mark, proving its enduring appeal. The decade ended with more advances being made with the flagship vehicle through the Porsche 964, which was intended to bring much of the new technology seen in vehicles such as the 959 to the iconic 911. Compared to the 911 Carrera, Porsche claimed the 964 had 85 per cent new parts and dubbed it the 'Carrera 4'. A rear-wheel drive version – the Carrera 2 – soon followed, as well as offering cabriolet and coupé versions to give consumers maximum choice.

Porsche did a lot of growing up through the 1980s thanks to a continued stream of well-received vehicles, as well as permeating further into mainstream media. But its most emphatic success had come on the racetrack, where it had created a new legacy at Le Mans across multiple cars and regulations, and had even seen its F1 efforts finally hit a high point. Off-track though, there were some choppy waters ahead that would prove difficult to navigate.

RIGHT: The 964 marked a significant update for the 911, featuring 85 per cent new parts.

REVIVAL MEETS RIVALRY

PORSCHE'S BOOM

As Porsche neared the new millennium, it found itself at a difficult crossroads. While many of its models had proved popular among consumers, there simply weren't enough of them, particularly in the United States.

Interest was waning chiefly due to the sizeable price tags involved and the influx of new, cheaper models from other German manufacturers such as Mercedes and BMW, and particularly in Japan, where cost-efficient approaches to manufacturing had left Porsche trailing behind.

The Porsche 968 was launched at the Frankfurt Motor Show in 1991 with a view to becoming the new entry model, taking over from the Porsche 944. The 944 had undergone a number of updates since its initial launch 10 years earlier, and while there was some carry-over to the 968, the fact that 80 per cent of the parts were new meant Porsche saw fit to christen this all-new model. The 968 also featured an upgraded 3-litre engine capable of producing 236 bhp. In a bid to cut costs, manufacturing of the

OPPOSITE: Heading into the new millennium, the 911 would continue to remain Porsche's prize model.

ABOVE: The Porsche 968 felt like too little, too late for Porsche as it tried to catch up with its front-engined rivals.

968 was also moved from the Audi plants back to Porsche's own factory at Zuffenhausen.

Yet it wasn't enough to make a dent in the market for front-engine sports cars, which was being dominated by Porsche's rivals. By now, Porsche was close to bankruptcy. Its manufacturing methods weren't keeping up with the rest of the automotive industry, and while the 911 remained popular, the 15,000 units it was shipping each year definitely wasn't enough to sustain the company. The family remained uneasy about the prospect of selling despite interest from bigger manufacturers such as Toyota.

The appointment of Wendelin Wiedeking as the new chairman of Porsche in 1993 proved to be an important turning point. Wiedeking was a tough taskmaster, showing little sympathy for wasted time or inefficiency, casting decisions often with a cigar hanging from his mouth. He quickly looked to Japan for new concepts when it came to running a manufacturing plant, drafting in designers from Toyota to try and teach those at Porsche their methods. It was a move that didn't go down well with much of Porsche's workforce, but the results soon had the desired effect. Assembly times were slashed and fewer errors were made, setting Porsche up for the purple patch that would follow.

Wiedeking's intolerance for underperforming models was a death knell for the 928 and the 968, both of which had ceased

LEFT: The appointment of Wendelin Wiedeking would be an important turning point for Porsche, which had neared financial oblivion.

ABOVE: The Porsche 993 remains the most iconic version of the 911, standing the test of time.

production by the end of 1995. By now, focus had shifted back towards the Porsche 911. The newest edition launched in 1994 was known as the Porsche 993, which would be the last air-cooled 911 but one that promised a significant number of technical advances.

To this day, the 993 stakes a claim to being the best-loved version of the 911. The early plans were laid in 1989 to develop a successor for the 964 model, the success of which meant there were certain elements that could be carried over, including the 3.6-litre engine. English designer Tony Hatter was tasked with overseeing the design of the 993, which retained the basic architecture of the 911 that was so iconic, whilst making tweaks such as adding more flared wheel arches and introducing seamless front and rear bumper designs. The 993 quickly won over the public who immediately fell for the 911's new look and sales boomed, prompting subsequent introductions of the Turbo (1995) and Targa (1996) editions.

The 993 also graced the Formula 1 circuit through 1995, being used as the safety car throughout the season, which was a rare major on-track appearance for Porsche around this time. Motor sport interests had been scaled back compared to the heyday of the 1980s. That was not to say there was not success, though. In 1994, more than a decade after its debut at the Daytona 24 Hours, the Porsche 962 powered to victory once again at the 24 Hours of Le Mans, albeit in unusual fashion. Jochen Dauer, a German fashion magnate, unveiled a road-legal version of the 962 at Frankfurt in 1993, featuring two seats and number plates that would allow it to comply with the new global regulations for GT racing. The car was entered as a Dauer 962 and beat Toyota to victory by one lap, giving Porsche its first win at Le Mans for seven years.

Road car plans were accelerating rapidly around this time as Porsche moved into new territory. While the 968 was being ushered out, there remained a desire to introduce something that would tick all the boxes as an entry-level Porsche: fun,

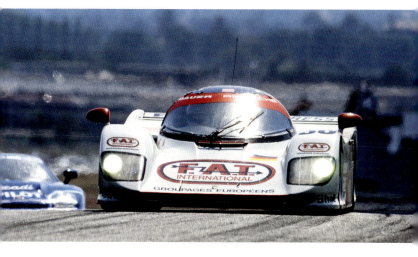

BELOW: A loophole in the regulations paved the way for the Porsche 962 to reign at Le Mans again, in 1994.

sporty and affordable. It prompted Porsche to go down the route of producing a mid-engined roadster, having seen the success of the Mazda MX-5, while retaining the sleek design and aesthetics it was renowned for. American designer Grant Larson was charged with the exterior design for a new concept car that would ultimately become the Porsche Boxster.

The Boxster had notes of iconic Porsches of old, such as the 550 Spyder, which was the most recent roadster it had designed. But the Boxster was very modern both outside (featuring a curved door and LED headlights) and in (with an LCD screen in the centre console). The two-seater concept was due to be unveiled at the Geneva Motor Show in 1993, only for this to be moved up to Detroit where the Boxster became the talk of the town. It was a major moment for Porsche, making a big splash in the United States where it had struggled for a number of years, and would be the catalyst to push on with plans to develop the concept into its latest model that would finally go on sale in 1996.

The Boxster would be the car that really ended Porsche's financial concerns, taking it firmly into the 21st century. The push for efficiency was aided by the Boxster's ability to share development with the 996 – the successor to the 993 – cutting costs for both models, as well as sharing parts with Toyota. Booming sales also helped: once the Boxster hit the US market, the price point of $40,000 made it an instant success and Porsche's best-selling car.

Porsche was now back in good health. In 1996, it celebrated the construction of the one millionth car.

RIGHT: The Porsche Boxster prototype was unveiled to great acclaim in 1993 – but took three more years to go on sale.

REVIVAL MEETS RIVALRY 109

ABOVE: Tweaks made the Porsche 996 a significant step forward for the 911 range, doing away with air-cooled designs.

As well as seeing the Boxster reach North America in 1997, Porsche launched the 996 one year later that was the first all-new edition of the 911 since the model debuted over 30 years earlier. It was the first 911 to use a liquid-cooled engine, marking a big shift for Porsche away from air-cooled designs. The car had also undergone weight reduction and had a more powerful 3.4-litre engine, blowing the vastly popular 993 out of the water.

In 1998 came the 50th anniversary of the first Porsche-badged car being produced, but it was not all celebrations: two and a half months earlier, Ferry Porsche had passed away at the age of 88. He had retired from involvement with the company in 1989 and lived out his final days at his cherished residence in Zell am See, where he was buried. It was a moment of reflection for Porsche. In Ferry, it had lost the patriarch who had kept it afloat and continued his father's legacy.

But the company was now standing strong yet again, enjoying strong commercial success – net profits doubled to $166m in 1998 – and retaining its strong cultural relevance. Porsche found its way into a plot line of the American sitcom *Friends* in 1999. An episode surrounded Joey Tribbiani finding the keys to a 996 version of the 911, prompting him to pretend it was his after impressing passers-by. After the owner claims back the keys, Joey keeps up the pretence by buying Porsche merchandise and pretending the 996 was under covers – only for it to turn out to be a collection of cardboard boxes. It also featured Joey delivering the iconic line: "Hey! It's Porsh-A!" when someone mispronounces the car's name as "Porsh" – a common misconnection the show did wonders to clear up.

But Porsche still needed to find new avenues if it wanted to keep up with other car manufacturers, prompting it to explore producing its own SUV. Initially announced in 1998 under the

ABOVE: Porsche began to explore a move into more family-friendly vehicles by designing an SUV prototype that would later become the Cayenne.

OPPOSITE: Porsche's high-performance roots were never lost, best reflected by the Porsche Carrera GT supercar that retailed for $440,000.

code name 'Colorado', Porsche set to work on the new car by renting a factory in Hemmingen, owing to the lack of space at its Weissach base. In 2002, the Porsche Cayenne was formally presented to the world. A first SUV – and, for that matter, a first car with four doors – was a big diversion for the sports car company, yet it went a long way to secure its future as consumers quickly made it the best-selling Porsche.

That wasn't to say Porsche had lost its roots. As exciting as the 959 had been, it was hardly a success, putting any ideas of a high-performance supercar on ice for a little while. In 2000, Porsche revealed a concept for a new limited production car. At its heart was a 5.5-litre V10 engine that had origins in its failed F1 project and had been earmarked for a Le Mans programme, only for that plan to be scrapped. The revenue from the success of the Cayenne meant Porsche could pursue plans for the new supercar, which would go on to become the Carrera GT. It was unveiled in 2004 on a limited production run that, while planned to reach 1,500, only got to 1,270 due to a change in

ABOVE: Upgrades to the 911 kept coming thick and fast, including a high-performance GT3 model.

US airbag regulations. The retail price of $440,000 didn't put o consumers who quickly raved about the Carrera GT's pioneerin motor sport technology and supreme performance. It is still widely regarded as one of the greatest supercars of the 2000s.

This pursuit of performance was also permeating into the other Porsche models, including the classic 911. A new edition, the 997, was launched in 2004, while the GT3 moniker had now been given to the high-performance versions of the 911. Porsche also continued to build on the success of the Boxster by launching a coupé version known as the Cayman, which shared the same chassis and engine.

But Porsche's continued success through the 2000s was set against the backdrop of continual power struggles. Ferdinand Piëch, the grandson of Ferdinand Porsche, had by now risen to become the head of Volkswagen, with whom Porsche had frequently collaborated and owned a 51 per cet share in. Volkswagen had by now boomed to incorporate a number of

Europe's leading luxury carmakers, including Lamborghini, Bentley and Bugatti. Wiedeking, the architect of Porsche's revival, had designs on increasing the company's influence.

It led to a boardroom battle where Wiedeking, the man who had saved Porsche in the early 1990s, pushed for a takeover of Volkswagen. But as the recession of the late 2000s bit and debts mounted for Porsche, Wiedeking's position became untenable, leading to his exit and paving the way for Volkswagen to take over Porsche instead. Piëch, who had always retained a shareholding in Porsche, had won the fight for control of the company he had walked out on in 1972.

The tussles did little to derail Porsche's continual commercial strength. The Boxster and Cayenne underwent updates through the 2000s, while the success of the SUV prompted Porsche to try and broaden its appeal further with a

BELOW: A tussle for power at Porsche ended in Ferdinand Piëch returning to control the company bearing his grandfather's name.

BELOW: The broadening appeal of Porsche continued with the launch of the Panamera, a four-door saloon.

four-door saloon, called the Panamera, that was launched in 2009.

Despite all this commercial success, Porsche wasn't pursuing a top-line motor sport programme. Audi was dominating Le Mans, which Porsche had failed to win since 1998 when it entered a GT1 version of the 911. The 911 GT3 was a dominant force in GT racing circles, winning four consecutive Nürburgring 24 Hours between 2006 and 2009, yet there was still an itch to scratch with prototypes.

Times were changing. The automotive industry was now starting to become more considerate of future technologies, such as hybrid and electricity. Porsche had already shown its willingness to divert from its core traditions with models such as the Boxster and the Cayenne, and had reaped the rewards handsomely. In fact, it's fair to say that they helped save Porsche. It would show the value of such a mentality and set the tone for the rapid change that was to follow as the 2010s began.

THE RETURN TO LE MANS

HYBRID HEYDAY

The changing automotive landscape through the mid-2000s meant a pivot to hybrid technology was always on the horizon for Porsche. It had always been a concept that had merit – the 1902 'Lohner-Porsche Mixte', which combined an electric wheel hub with a petrol engine, was a hybrid – but technology was now advancing to a level that it could be used in mass vehicle production.

Porsche first announced plans for a hybrid version of the Cayenne at the Frankfurt Motor Show in 2005, vaunting 'emission-free motoring' when in the fully electric mode while at low speeds and parking, as well as cutting fuel consumption by an estimated 15 per cent. A functioning version of a hybrid Cayenne was showcased in 2007, but it would not be for another three years until the Cayenne S Hybrid was formally launched. The 3-litre V6 Audi engine combined with an electric motor to provide 325 bhp, and a 0-60 mph time comparable with the Boxster – not bad going for an SUV. The exterior of the Cayenne was also given a facelift ahead of the hybrid version's launch.

OPPOSITE: Hybrid engineering went into the stunning 919, built to compete in the World Endurance Championship LMP1 class from 2014.

Hybrid technology was a good match for Porsche's cars with a broader appeal, making the Panamera as being ripe for a similar move. The plan for a hybrid version was announced in 2008 before the base model had even launched. The Panamera S Hybrid used the same drivetrain as the Cayenne S Hybrid, and immediately became the most environmentally friendly car in Porsche's range upon its launch in 2013, while still being capable of speeds of almost 170 mph.

The marriage between technology and performance was exactly what prompted Porsche to explore a return to prototype racing and competing for top honours at the 24 Hours of Le

Mans. In 2011, Porsche confirmed it would be reviving a works programme in the top flight of sports car racing, starting in 2014. Audi and Peugeot had become the dominant forces with their diesel-powered prototypes, but Porsche was always angling for hybrid technology to give it an edge over the competition.

It tallied with Porsche's plans for a new high-performance supercar that would also harness hybrid power, known as the Porsche 918 Spyder. Plans for the 918 were announced in 2010 at the Geneva Motor Show, where it was presented as being the road-going version of the RS Spyder sports car that had raced in the American Le Mans Series with great success.

BELOW: Plug-in hybrid technology was something Porsche went big on without sacrificing performance.

BELOW: The Porsche 919 Hybrid was unveiled ahead of the return to Le Mans under the new LMP1 hybrid rules in 2014.

Yet LMP1 was always where Porsche's heart had to lie if it wanted to recapture overall success at Le Mans and add to its tally of 16 outright victories. In June 2013, its new prototype hit the track for the first time, making use of two hybrid systems along with a petrol engine. Later that year, its name was revealed as the Porsche 919 Hybrid in a nod to Porsche's tradition at Le Mans and success with the 917, while also highlighting the links to the 918 Spyder.

Three years after the 918 Spyder concept had first been revealed, and two years after Porsche had started taking orders for the new supercar, the maiden production version of the car was presented at the Frankfurt Motor Show. The starting price

124 THE RETURN TO LE MANS

ABOVE: The Porsche 918 Spyder was an immediate sensation and became one of the greatest hypercars in the automotive world.

was $845,000, and only 918 units would ever be produced, selling out by the end of 2014.

The result of Porsche's hard work and just the fourth legitimate supercar it had ever produced was nothing short of spectacular. The 918 Spyder pushed the boundaries of new technologies in cars, harnessing a rear-axle steering system to ensure it kept the renowned agility and feel of a Porsche despite the added weight of the hybrid systems.

The car could run in an all-electric mode up to a top speed of 93 mph, albeit only to a range of 16 miles, and offered a variety of different modes all the way up to 'hot lap' for maximum performance. Combined with the 4.6-litre V8 engine that sang out of top-mounted exhausts, the hybrid system helped lift output to 875 bhp, a 0-60 time of 2.6 seconds and a top speed of 211 mph. *Top Gear* presenter Richard Hammond described the instant performance as being like "a sprinter falling out of bed and going straight into a world record".

BELOW: The Porsche Macan was launched in 2014, and has since become the best-selling model out of Weissach.

It cemented Porsche's place among the new era of hypercar royalty. The 918 Spyder joined Ferrari's La Ferrari and the McLaren P1 in the 'holy trinity' of hypercars released around the same time, and was also a taste of what Porsche had in store on the track with the 919 Hybrid that would first race at Le Mans in 2014.

But Porsche was not losing sight of its core clientele. The continued success of the Cayenne prompted it to further its interest in SUVs, launching a five-door luxury crossover SUV in 2014. The Macan – initially known internally as the Cajun, standing for 'Cayenne Junior' – was designed with the intention of offering sports car performance and retaining Porsche's DNA but with the practicality of an SUV. Today, it is Porsche's best-selling model.

Porsche had also revamped the 911 around this time. In 2011, the new 991 version of its classic model was revealed, and was only the third all-new edition of the 911 (after the original and the 996). It had a longer wheelbase but took plenty of Porsche's on-track learnings to result in a far more powerful car. The introduction of electric power steering meant the 911 had a different feel to its predecessors, yet its handling won great acclaim.

Porsche also gave a nod to the history of the 911 as it celebrated 50 years of its most iconic model in 2013. To celebrate, a special 50th anniversary edition of the 911 was commissioned and limited to 1,963 units. It was based on the very best of the new 991 and had an array of extras including 20-inch alloy wheels and a special '911 50' badge on the rear.

BELOW: Nearing 50 years of the Porsche 911, another update arrived in 2011 – the 991 – that took its power to the next level.

The hype was growing throughout this period for Porsche's return to Le Mans. After formally presenting the 919 Hybrid at the Geneva Motor Show in March 2014, the car made its racing debut at the 6 Hours of Silverstone, the opening round of the FIA World Endurance Championship. The series was formed in 2012 with Le Mans as its centrepiece and saw Porsche enter its pair of 919 Hybrids against cars from Audi and Toyota in the premier LMP1 class.

However, 2014 was a difficult first year for the 919 Hybrid. While it was quick over a single lap, scoring three pole positions, sustaining the challenge to Audi and Toyota over the long race distances proved more of a challenge. A maiden victory arrived in São Paulo with Romain Dumas, Neel Jani and Marc Lieb, but the race was marred by a huge crash in the second car for ex-Formula 1 driver Mark Webber, who thankfully escaped unharmed.

BELOW: Porsche's return to the top level at Le Mans in 2014 didn't bring immediate success, but the trophies would soon follow.

Porsche made its intentions clear for 2015, announcing plans to enter a third 919 Hybrid to Le Mans in a bid to end its win drought. Updates to the car included a lighter chassis and an improved hybrid system, while F1 star Nico Hülkenberg was drafted in to race in the third car alongside Porsche factory drivers Nick Tandy and Earl Bamber.

Signs of progress in 2015 were immediately noticeable as Porsche took the fight to Audi at Silverstone, losing by just four seconds over a six-hour race. Victory proved elusive again at Spa, but at Le Mans, the 919's supremacy soon shone through. Porsche took a 1-2-3 in qualifying, led by Neel Jani on pole position. Yet come the race, it was the third car that came to the fore. A magical night stint by Tandy set the number 19 Porsche crew on course for victory, leaving it to Hülkenberg to cross the line and give Porsche its first outright 24 Hours of Le Mans victory for 18 years.

ABOVE: Brendon Hartley, Mark Webber and Timo Bernhard celebrate winning the World Endurance Championship in 2015.

ABOVE: A staged finish for Porsche in June 2015 as it secures its first outright win at Le Mans for 18 years.

It would not be Tandy's only shock success in 2015. Porsche retained a factory presence in GT racing with its Porsche 911 RSR in the IMSA SportsCar Championship, based in the United States. In the rain-shortened season finale at Road Atlanta known as 'Petit Le Mans', Porsche pulled off one of the biggest upsets in modern sports car racing history as Tandy and team-mate Patrick Pilet made use of the GT car's greater grip in the wet to defeat the faster prototypes, securing the overall win.

Porsche capped off an enormously successful year on the track by clinching its first World Endurance Championship titles, with the drivers' crown being shared by Webber, Timo

Bernhard and Brendon Hartley. The 919 Hybrid had been on pole for every single race of the eight-round season.

Porsche would win again at Le Mans in 2016, albeit with a huge slice of luck. Toyota was on course to score its first Le Mans win, leading by over a minute entering the final stages before a technical issue on its car caused it to stop on the final lap. The number 2 919 Hybrid of Lieb, Jani and Dumas picked up the pieces to give Porsche an unlikely 18th overall win at Le Mans, paving the way for the trio to also win the WEC title.

The last competitive hurrah for the 919 Hybrid came in 2017. The spiralling costs of the LMP1 programme, the appeal

OVERLEAF: The Porsche 919 Hybrid would be retired after 2017, signing off with a third Le Mans win in a row.

of the new all-electric Formula E series and the fallout from the Dieselgate scandal that engulfed the VW Group meant the purse strings had to be tightened. Porsche gave the car a fitting swansong as it won a third straight Le Mans, this time with Bamber, Hartley and Bernhard, who recovered from spending almost one hour in the garage to score victory in a race of attrition that saw all of the LMP1 cars hit trouble. Porsche announced one month later it would be quitting LMP1 at the end of the year, but signed off with another set of championships ahead of Toyota.

Yet there would be one more year of fun for the 919 Hybrid, which in addition to its enormous success had also showcased Porsche's capabilities with hybrid technology and helped further advancements for its road cars. Porsche announced it would be holding a 919 Tribute Tour through 2018, visiting a number of the world's most iconic racetracks and embarking on some special record attempts to provide a fitting send-off.

Without the restrictions of the WEC's technical regulations, the Porsche 919 Hybrid Evo was more powerful than its base model and made use of active aerodynamics to offer more downforce and less drag on the straights. Jani's attempt at Spa was 12 seconds faster than Porsche's 2017 time, and even beat Lewis Hamilton's Formula 1 pole position lap. But the bigger prize would come at the Nürburgring's fearsome Nordschleife layout, where Jani recorded a lap of 5m 19.546s to smash the existing record set by Stefan Bellof in a Porsche 956 in 1983 by almost a minute. But as it was not a lap set in a competitive event, the record was sadly unofficial.

While Porsche's on-track efforts with hybrid technology had come to an end, they remained central to its range of road cars. The Cayenne S E-Hybrid was launched in 2014, becoming the third plug-in hybrid Porsche after the Panamera and the 918 Spyder, as well as being the first plug-in hybrid SUV on the market. Away from its hybrid range, Porsche had to react to increasing clampdowns on engine size and output in Europe, leading to the launch of two new turbocharged models in 2017. The 718 Boxster and the 718 Cayman gave a nod to the 718 racing car from the late 1950s and still packed a punch to appeal to the traditional Porsche audience.

Porsche had returned and conquered at Le Mans, proving its hybrid prowess. But just as it had to react quickly when the industry became enamoured with that technology, it now had to keep up with the shift away from the combustion engine altogether, taking it back to the very start of its story.

BELOW: The 718 Boxster gave a clear nod to Porsche's past while its design moved the model into the future.

OVERLEAF: Porsche now boasted a range of cars that ticked the box for almost every type of consumer.

ELECTRIC
DREAMS

INTO THE
FUTURE

When Ferdinand Porsche became fascinated with electrification as a teenager in the 1890s, experimenting in the Vratislavice family home with whatever he could get his hands on, there was no way of knowing it would lead to such a dynasty bearing his name.

Even more remarkable was that 110 years later, Porsche found itself facing a similar consideration of just what possibilities electric technology could offer amid a seismic shift within the automotive industry. In the early 2010s, it was clear that electric cars were an avenue all manufacturers had to go down.

Porsche saw the way the wind was blowing and took its first steps towards producing an all-electric car by unveiling a new concept called 'Mission E' at the Frankfurt Motor Show in 2015. One look at the Mission E car was enough to tell you it was a Porsche, retaining the iconic sloping front that had an even lower profile than normal given the lack of an engine. Technology from the Porsche 919 Hybrid that had won at Le Mans was at the heart of the Mission E, which was intended to carry design notes of

OPPOSITE: Porsche's plans for an all-electric car were first announced in 2015 with the bold 'Mission E' concept.

ABOVE: The Mission E was well received, but the final version, the Taycan, would not quite reach the ambition of the concept car.

a race car from the outside as well. The four-door Mission E concept was well received, prompting the Porsche board to give the green light later that year to go ahead with designing an all-electric production car.

The result would be the Porsche Taycan, its name translating from Turkish as 'spirited young horse', the animal at the heart of the Porsche crest. Porsche made plans to pour more than €6 billion into the development of electric cars by 2025, knowing the significance that electric cars would come to have in the future, particularly with the ability to cross over parts and manufacturing with the other Volkswagen brands.

The need to think beyond Porsche alone meant the Taycan couldn't quite live up to the futuristic design the Mission E had teased. It was instead a four-door saloon, in keeping with the practicality models such as the Cayenne had offered.

But Porsche wanted to make clear that it had not skimped on performance. In late 2018, Porsche completed a 24-hour test that saw the Taycan complete 2,128 miles at an average speed of 88.7 mph. The drivers would push at a speed of over 120 mph, drain the battery, fast-charge it and repeat the process. In the summer of 2019, just months before the car's launch, the Taycan set a lap time of 7m 42s around the Nürburgring's Nordschleife layout, just two seconds off the Porsche 997 from 2009. It wasn't bad for a two-tonne electric car.

The Taycan proved popular upon release, surpassing Porsche's targets and accounting for over 10 per cent of its sales by the end of 2020. Coming in at a cheaper price point than both the Panamera and the 911, the base Taycan model was still capable of just over 400 bhp. But a range of models were released to satisfy those seeking more performance, including the Taycan Turbo and the Taycan Turbo S – peculiar names, given the lack of any turbocharger… with the latter enjoying

BELOW: The futuristic interior of the Taycan spoke of the car being the next generation of Porsches.

TAYCAN

ABOVE: The Porsche Taycan was a radical solution that promised not to scrimp on performance, producing more than 750bhp.

a peak output of more than 750 bhp and a 0-60 mph time of 2.6 seconds. Owners could charge the cars overnight at home, while the Taycan could reach 80 per cent battery level in just over 20 minutes using an 800-volt charging station.

Porsche's need to play big on its electric push was partly due to the Dieselgate scandal that had engulfed the Volkswagen Group. VW was found to have fitted illegal software in around 11 million of its diesel vehicles that was designed to cheat emissions tests, leading to more than €30 billion in fines. While Porsche was not directly impacted, it nevertheless forced the whole VW Group to place an increased focus on electrification in a bid to clean up its image.

The emergence of the Dieselgate scandal came around the same time that Porsche underwent a change in management. Oliver Blume, a member of Porsche's executive board, took

ABOVE: Oliver Blume took over as Porsche CEO in 2015, and made it clear that the company's roots would not be sacrificed.

over as CEO of the company in 2015, and was clear in the need to focus on electric and hybrid solutions. But he stressed that Porsche "will always be a sports car brand" and there would be no compromise on performance, even as new mobility methods were explored.

The impact of Dieselgate also stretched to the reputation of Ferdinand Piëch. His strict culture at Volkswagen and refusal to accept failure had helped turn the fortunes of the carmaker around and helped create the empire that ultimately acquired Porsche. Yet his approach was also seen by some as the root of the push to cheat the emission tests. Piëch always denied involvement in the matter. Amid boardroom battles at Volkswagen with CEO Martin Winterkorn, Piëch retired from the board in 2015, but remained active in the company until his final days, passing away suddenly at the age of 82 in 2019. Blume led Porsche's tributes to Piëch, thanking him for the "passion and the courage with which he led Porsche to outstanding engineering achievements".

Porsche's push towards electrification was part of the rationale behind the decision to close the successful Le Mans prototype programme at the end of 2017, less than four years after the 919 Hybrid had made its competitive debut. The announcement of the programme's closure was accompanied by news that Porsche would be entering Formula E from 2019. The all-electric series started in 2014, staging street races in city centres, and had attracted a number of major manufacturers including Mercedes, Jaguar, Nissan, Audi and BMW. The entry marked Porsche's return to single-seater racing after more than two decades away.

The staff working on the LMP1 programme pivoted to the new Formula E operation, laying the foundations for the team to debut in Saudi Arabia at the end of 2019. Using a spec chassis supplied to all teams, Porsche developed its own all-electric powertrain capable of producing speeds up to 174 mph when in its full power 250kW mode for qualifying laps. Former LMP1 drivers Neel Jani and Andre Lotterer were signed to race for the team, with the latter scoring a second place finish on debut in the Porsche 99X Electric car.

Success in Formula E would prove hard to come by. The competitive nature of the series made it tricky for new teams to taste success right away, limiting Porsche to just two podiums in its debut season. A first win looked to have been secured in Mexico by Pascal Wehrlein, a new signing for 2020, only for the German driver to be disqualified for a tyre infringement. Porsche would make up for it one year later in emphatic fashion as Wehrlein led home Lotterer for a 1-2 finish in front of a packed crowd at the Autodromo Hermanos Rodriguez in Mexico City, marking its first Formula E victory.

OPPPOSITE: Porsche entered Formula E in 2019 with its first all-electric racing car, the 99X.

ABOVE: Even after quitting LMP1, Porsche continued to taste success at Le Mans with its GTE-Pro entries, seen here in classic liveries.

While the 919 Hybrid programme may have ended, Porsche still retained a presence at Le Mans through its GT racing efforts. The Porsche 911 RSR was still going strongly, with an updated version that was launched in 2017 being hailed as "the biggest evolution in the history" of the 911 as it switched to a mid-engined layout. The car would sweep to a dominant 1-2 in the GTE-Pro class at Le Mans in 2018, the winning number 92 decked out in the classic 'Pink Pig' livery that had adorned the 917/20 back in 1971. The victory set up drivers Michael Christensen and Kevin Estre to also win the GTE drivers' title in the World Endurance Championship.

It only added to the enduring legend of the Porsche 911, the road-going version of which was also undergoing further updates. In November 2018, Porsche unveiled the 992-generation 911, which brought back some of the classic design elements the iconic 993 had been so loved for some 20 years earlier. The curvy nature of the 993 had been lost as

Porsche took the 911 down a more Boxster-style aerodynamic route through the 2000s, but it made a welcome return with the wider body styled for the 992, which was the first edition of the 911 to be fully designed under Volkswagen's ownership of Porsche.

The 992 was initially launched with Carrera S and 4S at the end of 2018, but further models followed. This included the Targa, which was given a special Heritage Design Edition by Porsche that was intended to take lucky owners back to the 1950s and 1960s, complete with a retro badge and corduroy interior.

For those keen on the maximum road-legal performance available from the latest 911, the 992 GT3 remained the pinnacle. While the 4-litre flat-six engine had been carried over from the 991, its output surpassing 500 bhp, improved

BELOW: The Porsche 992 GT3 is the peak of road-legal performance offered in the 911 range.

ABOVE: Porsche 911s remain a staple in endurance races throughout the world, seen here in the 24 Hours of Barcelona.

aerodynamics that doubled the downforce available made the new GT3 the ultimate track-ready version of the 911 upon its release in 2021.

Electric mobility had become a focus for Porsche, but its continued efforts with the 911 proved it was not the only solution moving forward. The manufacturer remained eager to offer a range of cars and power solutions to please all customers, ensuring its relevance. A range of different Taycan models quickly followed the base editions, including the bigger Cross Turismo, while the Cayenne was given a total update in 2018. It remains one of the best-selling Porsche models.

With hybrids still selling strongly and showing little sign of waning in interest, Porsche began to mull over fighting for top honours at Le Mans once again. Measures had been taken following the departure of both Porsche and Audi to make the premier prototype class more appealing, leading to its

rebranding as Le Mans Hypercar. Officials in the United States were keen for a formula in the IMSA series that could also race at Le Mans, leading to the creation of Le Mans Daytona h (LMDh), a class that would keep costs down by using a spec-hybrid system and a base chassis. Porsche announced in December 2020 that it would return to prototype racing via the new class in conjunction with Penske from 2023.

News of Porsche's plan to return to Le Mans was met warmly, particularly amid the influx of manufacturers such as Peugeot, Ferrari, Audi and Acura to the newly formed classes. It has the potential to set up a new golden age of sports car racing and give Porsche the opportunity to add to its record tally of 19 overall wins at the Circuit de la Sarthe. Formula 1 is also something that continues to pique the interest of Weissach officials given the series' commitment to hybrid technology and the push to use synthetic fuels moving forward.

ABOVE: Porsche will return to the top class at Le Mans in 2023 with a new LMDh car, tested here in a camouflage livery.

Despite the impact of the Covid-19 pandemic, Porsche enjoyed a record year of sales in 2021 as it delivered over 300,000 vehicles to customers for the first time. Sales in the United States were up by almost a quarter, with the top-selling model being the Macan. Blume had claimed that Porsche would "always be a sports car brand", and while that DNA applies to every single car produced, Porsche is also now so much more than that. It caters to family outings and high-speed track days – and everything in between.

An astonishing statistic is that two-thirds of all Porsches ever made are still on the road. It is testament to not only the incredible reliability of the Porsche cars, but also their enduring appeal. While some models may be more loved than others, Porsche's standards have always been exceptionally high – right from the humble beginnings when it was Ferdinand Porsche's family business.

Porsche has navigated world wars, family feuds and boardroom battles, diced with going bust and enjoyed huge booms. Its history may be turbulent, but more than 70 years after the first true Porsche rolled out of that humble sawmill in Gmünd, it is now one of the world's best-loved manufacturers. It is a symbol for everything we love about cars.

Let's face it: nothing quite compares to a Porsche.

OPPOSITE: Sales continue to reach record highs year-on-year as Porsche retains its place among the world's greatest carmakers.

BELOW: The iconic badge remains a hallmark of quality, reliability and performance.

OVERLEAF: Porsche's future is looking brighter than ever thanks to its wide range of vehicles.

INDEX

(Key: **bold** indicates text includes accompanying photographs, *italic* refers to all other photos/captions)

A

aerodynamics 16, 86, 94, 134, 149, 150
all-electric series 134, 146, *146*
Attwood, Richard 68
Audi 77, 78, 104, 116, 121, 123, 128, 129, 146, 150, 151
Austro-Daimler 13–15
Auto Union 17, 18, *18*, 19, *19*
Autodromo Hermanos Rodriguez 146

B

Bamber, Earl 129, 134
bankruptcy 104
Barnard, John 88
Barth, Edgar 41
Behra, Jean 41
Bell, Derek 85–6
Bellof, Stefan 86, *87*, 134
Bernhard, Timo *129*, 130–1, 134
Blume, Oliver **144–6**
branding 17, 27, 31, 33, 49, 67, 86, 90, 142, 145, 151, **153–5**

C

Can-Am 71–2, **73**
Cayenne **112**, 115, 117, 121–2
Christensen, Michael 148
Circuit de la Sarthe 36, 61, 151
Cisitalia 27–9, 31
Cisitalia Type 360 23
'Colorado' SUV 111–12
C.2 Phaeton **11**

D

Daimler-Motoren-Gesellschaft 15
Dakar Rally *94*
Dauer, Jochen 107
Daytona 24 Hours 60, 61–2, 74, *74*, 107, 151, *151*
Dean, James **37–9**
Dennis, Ron 87
Dieselgate 134, 144–5
Donohue, Mark 72–3
Dr. Ing. h.c. F. Porsche GmbH 16
Dumas, Romain 128, 131

E

Egger **11**
electric cars 117, **120–37**, **140–55**
electrification 10–11, 33
Elford, Vic 60, **61–2**
Estre, Kevin 148

F

Fabi, Teo 91
family tensions 75–7, 114–15, *115*, 153
fashion symbols *56–7*, 62
Ferrari 60–1, 68, 89, 151
FIA 61, 74, 85, 128
50th anniversary 110
Follmer, George 72
Footwork 91
Ford 20, 60–1, 88
Formula E 134, **146**
Formula 1 (F1) 41–2, *42*, 53, 68, **85–91**, 98, 107, 128–9, 134
Frankfurt Motor Show 51, 103, 121, 124, 141
French Grand Prix **42**
Friends 111
Fuhrmann, Ernst 79–80

G

Geneva Motor Show 67, 79, 108, 123, 128
German Grand Prix 41
Glöckler, Helmut 37
Gmünd HQ 27, 31, 45, 75, 153
Golden Steering Wheel 80
Grands Prix (GP) **18–19**, 41, 42, *42*, 87
Gregg, Peter 74
Group B regulations *94*
Group C regulations 85–6
Group 5 regulations 67, 75, 78
Group 6 regulations 85
GT racing 60, 107, 130, 148

Gurney, Dan **42**

H
Hamilton, Lewis 134
Hammond, Richard 125
Hartley, Brendon *129*, 131, 134
Hatter, Tony 106
Haywood, Hurley 74
Hemmingen factory 112
Herrmann, Hans 41, 60, 68
High Performance Car Ltd 18
Hitler, Adolf **18–23**
Hochleistungsfahrzeugbau GmbH 18
Hoffman, Max 32
homologation 74
'hot lap' 125
Hülkenberg, Nici 129
Hunaudières Straight 79
hybrid technology **12–13**, 117, **121–37**, **140–55**

I
Ickx, Jacky 78, 85–6
IMSA 86, 90, 130, 151
Indianapolis 500 90

IndyCar **90–2**

J
Jacob Lohner and Co. 11–13
Jani, Neel 128, 129, 131, 134, 146

K
KdF-Wagen **21–3**
Knight Rider 95

L
La Sarthe circuit 36, 61, 151
Lamborghini 115
land speed *19*, 73
Larson, Grant 108
Lauda, Niki **88–90**
Le Mans **33–6**, 40–1, 59, 60, 62, **67–75**, 78–9, **84–7**, 93, 98, **107**, 112, 116, 122–4, **128–35**, 141, 146, 148, **150–1**
Le Mans **68–71**
Le Mans Daytona h 151
Lennep, Gijs van 71
Lieb, Marc 128, 131
'Little Bastard' **39**
LMDh class **151**

LMP1 class *121*, 124, 128, 131–4, 146, *148*
Lohner, Jacob 11
Lohner, Ludwig 9, **11–13**
Lohner-Porsche Mixte **12–13**, 121
Lotterer, Andre 146

M
MacGyver 95
McQueen, Steve **68–71**
Maglioli, Umberto 41
Marko, Helmut 71
Mercedes 15, 19, 103, 146
Mezger, Hans 88
Mission E **140–2**
'Moby Dick' 78–9
Model T (Ford) 20
models of Porsche:
  99X Electric **146–7**
  356 23, **27–37**, *32*, *36*, **44–5**, 49–57
  356/1 29–31
  356 C 56–7
  356 SL Coupe *33*
  356 SL Gmünd-Coupé 36

356 Speedster 32–3, 39
356 Super Speedster *37*
356, 10,000th 45
500 Spyder **38–9**, 108
550 36–7, 40, 41
550 roadster 37
550 Spyder *33*, *34–5*, 108
718 Boxster **135**
718 Cayman 135
718 RSK **39–42**, 135
804 42
901 **50–2**
904 42–5, *42*, *43*, 49, 51–3, 60
906 60
907 60, 62
908 61, 68
911 **49–54**, 57–8, *62*, *63*, **74**, **77–80**, **93–9**, *102*, *103*, **106**, **110–11**, 143, **148–50**
911 '911 50' 50th-anniversary edition **127**
911 GT1 116
911 GT3

INDEX 157

112–14, 116
911 RSR Carrera 74, 79, 95, 98, 130, 148
911 SC 80, 93
911 Targa 58–9, 106
911 Turbo 74–5, 80, 106
911R **59–60**
911S 58–60
911T **61–2**
912 **54–7**, 62, 76, 77–8
914 **62**
917 **67–73**, 74, 85, 124
917/20 **71**
917/30 72
917K *66*, *67*
918 Spyder **123–6**, 134
919 Hybrid *120*, *121*, **124**, 126, **128–33**, 141, 146, 148
919 Hybrid Tribute Tour 134
919 Hybrid Evo 134
924 *76–7*, 77–8, 80, 93
928 79, 105
930 75
935 75, 78, 86
935/78 78–9
936 78, **84–5**
936/81 85
936 Martini 78
944 **92–3**, 103
956 **85–8**
959 **93–5**, 98, 112
962 86, **107**
964 106
964 Carrera 2 98
964 Carrera 4 98
968 **103–8**
991 127, 149
992 148–9
992 Carrera 4S 149
992 Carrera S 149
992 GT3 **149–50**
992 Targa Heritage Design Edition 149
993 **106–7**, 148
996 **110–11**, 127
997 114
Boxster **108–10**, 115, 117, 121, 149
Boxster Cayman 114
Cajun, *see* Porsche Macan
Carrera GT **112–14**
Carrera GTS 51
Cayenne **112**, 115, 117, 121, 126, 142, 150
Cayenne S E-Hybrid 134
Cayenne S Hybrid 121, 122
Cross Turismo 150
GTE-Pro **148**
Macan **126**
Mixte **12–13**, 121
one millionth car 108
Panamera **116–17**
Panamera S Hybrid 122, 134, 143
P1 **11–12**
P-Wagen 18, 19
Taycan **142–4**, 150
Taycan Turbo 143
Taycan Turbo S 143–4
Type 12 17, *20*
Type 32 **16–17**, 20
Type 64 22, 29, 31
Type 754 T7 **49–50**
Monte Carlo Rally **61**, **79**
Motor Sport Magazine *80*, *81*
Mouche, Edmond *33*

N

Neerpasch, Jochen 60
'Nobody's Perfect' poster 86
Nordschleife circuit 86, *87*, 134, 143
Nürburgring Eifelrennen 37, 42, 60, 86, 116, 134, 143

P

Panamera **116–17**, 122
Paris Motor Show 32
people's car 18, 19–20
Petit Le Mans 130
Peugeot 51, *51*, 123, 151
Piëch, Anton (son-in-law) 16, 23
Pilet, Patrick 130
'pink pig' livery 71, *71*, 148
plug-in technology, *see* hybrid technology
Porsche models, *see under* models of Porsche
Porsche AG 76–7, 93
Porsche, Aloisia (wife) 15
Porsche, Anna (mother) 9, 10
Porsche, Anton (father) 9, 10
Porsche, Butzi (grandson) 31, 42, *44–5*, 45, *48*, 49, *49*, 52–3, 60, 77

Porsche Design 77
Porsche Doppelkupplung (PDK) 86
Porsche, Ferdinand 8, *9*, *13*, *17*, *26*, *31*, 53, 59, 76, 87, 114
  birth of 9, *10*
  career moves 13–15
  education and apprenticeship 10–11, 33, 141
  first car designs 11–13, 16–17, *20*, *22*, 45
  honorary doctorates 16
  legacy 110, *115*
  racing career 12, 13–15
  WWII imprisonment 23, *27*, 31, 75
Porsche, Ferdinand Alexander (grandson), *see* Porsche, Butzi
Porsche, Ferdinand Piëch (grandson) 31, *31*, 53, 59–61, 67–8, 72, 76, 77, *80*, 93, **114–15**, 145–6
Porsche, Ferry (son) **14–17**, 23, 27, 29, 31–2, **44–5**, 48, *49*, 50, 52–3, 57, *62*, *63*, **75–7**, 79, 110
Porsche, Louise (daughter) **14–15**, 27, 31, 76
Prinz Heinrich race 13–15
Prost, Alain 89–90, *89*

R

Rallye Monte Carlo **61**, **79**
Reutter 32, 45
Rosenberger, Adolf 18

S

Schutz, Peter 93
Seidel, Wolfgang 41
Siffert, Jo 61
Silver Arrows 19
Silverstone 128, *129*
6 Hours race 128
S-1500 class 37
Speedway 73
SportsCar 78, 90, 130
Steinemann, Rico 75
Stewart, Jackie 68
Stuck, Hans 87
Stuck, Hans-Joachim 87
Stuttgart factory 23, 31–3
SUVs 111–12, 115, 121, 126, 134–5

T

TAG-Porsche **88–90**
Talladega Speedway 73
Tandy, Nick 129–30
Targa Florio 15, 41, 58, 62
Techniques d'Avant Garde (TAG) **88–90**
Top Gear 125
Toyota 104, 105, 107, 108, 128, 131, 134
TV and film 37–9, 68–71, 95
24 Hours races 33–6, *33*, 60, 61–2, 74, *74*, 107, 122–4, *150*
2+2 design 50

U

University of Applied Sciences 15–16

V

V6 engine *88*, 121
V8 engine 79, 91, 125
V10 engine 112
V16 engine 19
Veuillet, Auguste *33*
Volkswagen (VW) *16*, **19–23**, 28, 33, 62, *62*, 78, 114–15, 134, 142, 149
VW Beetle 31
VW Group 134, 144–5

W

Webber, Mark 128, *129*, 130
Wehrlein, Pascal 146
Weissach factory 112, *126*, 151, *152*
Wiedeking, Wendelin **104–5**, 115
Winterkorn, Martin 145
Woolfe, John 68
World Endurance Championship (WEC) *121*, **128–34**, 148
World Exhibition, Paris 13
World War I 15
World War II 20, 22–3, *27*, 75
Wütherich, Rolf 39

Z

Zell am See 76, 110
Zuffenhausen factory 68, 104

CREDITS

The publishers would like to thank the following sources for their kind permission to reproduce the pictures in this book.

ALAMY: CTK 10; culture-images GmbH 113, 114; DAX Images 150; dpa picture alliance 11, 26, 44-45, 95, 116-117, 151; Ken Eastman 37; Heritage Image Partnership Ltd 19, 56-57; INTERFOTO 58; Iain Masterton 16; mauritius images GmbH 12; nawson 62; PictureLux/The Hollywood Archive 69; Shawshots 21, 32

GETTY IMAGES: Krisztian Bocsi/Bloomberg 140; CBS 34-35; Chesnot 135; Myung J. Chun/Los Angeles Times 4; Gerlach Delissen/Corbis 120; Tristan Fewings 22; Heinrich Hoffmann/Hulton Archive 23; ISC Images & Archives 74; Kasperski/ullstein bild 80; Thomas Kienzle/AFP 152; Martyn Lucy 52-53; National Motor Museum/Heritage Images 36; Porsche AG 112; Guenter Schiffmann/Bloomberg 115; ullstein bild 8, 30; Horacio Villalobos/Corbis 125

MARY EVANS PICTURE LIBRARY: Imagno 13

MOTORSPORT IMAGES: 87, 94, 96-97; Sam Bloxham/LAT 128, 129; Simon Galloway/LAT 147; Nikolaz Godet/LAT 132-133; David Hutson/LAT 90-91; LAT 18, 40-41, 43, 61, 79, 84, 107, 148; David Phipps/Sutton Images 51, 78; Rainer Schlegelmilch 54, 66, 70, 72-73, 75, 104, 106; Sutton Images 42, 88, 89, 130-131

PORSCHE AG: 14, 17, 33, 63, 102

SHUTTERSTOCK: 55, 127; Nina Alizada 28-29; Egon Bomsch/Imagebroker 76-77; czech wanderer 98-99; emirhankaramuk 136-137; Foto by M 126; josefkubes 71; Keystone/Zuma 48; Thomas Kienzle/AP 105; Dong liu 124; Magic Car Pics 81, 92, 110-111; mi_viri 50; North Monaco 154-155; Rich Pearce/Future 59; Richard Sheinwald/AP 108-109; Sipa 38; ben smith 153; Martial Trezzini/EPA-EFE 145; VanderWolf Images 122-123, 142, 144; Veyron Photo 143, 149

WIKIMEDIA COMMONS: 20

Every effort has been made to acknowledge correctly and contact the source and/or copyright holder of each picture any unintentional errors or omissions will be corrected in future editions of this book.